200
Cake Mix
Creations

Stephanie Ashcraft

D0952495

GIBBS SMITH
TO ENRICH AND INSPIRE HUMANKIND

For my family and friends. —S.A.

First Edition
15 14 13 12   10 9 8 7 6 5

Published by
Gibbs Smith
P.O. Box 667
Layton, Utah 84041

Orders: 1.800.748.5439
www.gibbs-smith.com

Designed by Debra McQuiston
Printed and bound in China
Gibbs Smith books are printed on either recycled, 100% post-
consumer waste, FSC-certified papers or on paper produced
from a 100% certified sustainable forest/controlled wood source.

Library of Congress Cataloging-in-Publication Data
Ashcraft, Stephanie.
  200 cake mix creations / Stephanie Ashcraft. — 1st ed.
     p. cm.
  ISBN-13: 978-1-4236-1705-1
  ISBN-10: 1-4236-1705-3
 1. Baking. 2. Cake. I. Title. II. Title: Two hundred cake mix
creations.
  TX763.A77 2010
  641.8'653—dc22
                                    2010006853

Contents

Helpful
Hints

1. Always beat cake batter with an electric mixer for at least 2 minutes.

2. Always grease and flour the cake pan, or spray it with oil—even when the recipe doesn't call for it.

3. Bake cakes on the middle oven rack, never on the top or bottom racks.

4. For chewier cookies and bars, take them out of the oven just as they begin to turn golden brown around the edges and let them cool on or in the pan.

5. For recipes using gelatin, make sure the gelatin is completely dissolved in hot water before adding any cold water.

6. When using fresh fruit, dip it in pineapple, orange, or lemon juice so it won't change color.

7. To see if a cake is done, insert a toothpick into the center—if it comes out clean, it's done. If the cake springs back when touched, that also means it's done.

8. The first time you try a recipe, check about 5 minutes before its minimum cooking time ends—each oven heats differently.

9. For best results, use glass or stoneware baking dishes.

10. Don't overbake anything, especially cookies and bars. Finished products should always be moist and chewy.

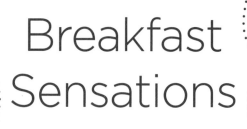

Breakfast Sensations

Easy Cinnamon Rolls

Makes **15** *rolls*

2¼ cups very
warm water
1 (0.25-ounce) envelope
or 2¼ teaspoons
active dry yeast
1 yellow or white
cake mix
5 cups flour
½ cup butter or
margarine, softened
1 cup firmly packed
brown sugar
2 teaspoons cinnamon
¼ cup raisins (optional)
1 container cream
cheese frosting

In a large bowl, mix together the water and yeast with a whisk. Whisk cake mix into yeast water. Stir in flour 1 cup at a time. Let dough stand in bowl in a draft-free place for 45 minutes. Punch down and then roll into an 18 x 10-inch rectangle. Add a small amount of flour if dough is too sticky while kneading.

In a separate bowl, mix together the butter, brown sugar, and cinnamon. Heat in the microwave for 15 seconds. Spread over rolled-out dough. Sprinkle raisins over top, if desired. Starting with widest end, roll dough into a tight log. Cut into 15 rolls and place cut side down in a greased 9 x 13-inch pan. Let rolls rise for about 25 minutes.

Preheat oven to 350 degrees. When heated, bake rolls for 19–23 minutes.

Warm the frosting in the microwave for 30–40 seconds and then drizzle desired amount over the baked rolls.

Orange Rolls

2¼ cups very
   warm water
1 (0.25-ounce) envelope
   or 2¼ teaspoons
   active dry yeast
1 yellow or white
   cake mix
2½ tablespoons grated
   orange rind, divided
5 cups flour
1 (8–ounce) package
   cream cheese,
   softened
½ cup sugar
1 cup powdered sugar
2 tablespoons orange
   juice

In a large bowl, mix together the water and yeast with a whisk. Whisk cake mix into yeast water. Stir in 1 tablespoon orange rind. Stir in flour 1 cup at a time. Let dough stand in bowl in a draft-free place for 45 minutes. Punch down and then roll into an 18 x 10-inch rectangle. Add a small amount of flour if dough is too sticky while kneading.

In a separate bowl, mix together the cream cheese, sugar, and remaining orange rind. Spread over rolled-out dough. Starting with widest end, roll dough into a tight log. Cut into 15 rolls and place cut side down in a greased 9 x 13-inch pan. Let rolls rise for about 25 minutes.

Preheat oven to 350 degrees. When heated, bake rolls for 19–23 minutes.

In a bowl, mix together the pow-dered sugar and orange juice until smooth. Spread over warm rolls.

Sticky Buns

Makes **15** buns

2¼ cups very
   warm water
1 (0.25-ounce) envelope
   or 2¼ teaspoons
   active dry yeast
1 yellow or white
   cake mix
5 cups flour
2 tablespoons butter or
   margarine, softened
½ cup sugar
2 teaspoons cinnamon
½ cup butter or
   margarine, melted
½ cup firmly packed
   brown sugar
1 cup chopped nuts

In a large bowl, mix together the water and yeast with a whisk. Whisk cake mix into yeast water. Stir in flour 1 cup at a time. Let dough stand in bowl in a draft-free place for 45 minutes. Punch down and then roll into an 18 x 10-inch rectangle. Add a small amount of flour if dough is too sticky while kneading.

Spread 2 tablespoons softened butter over rolled-out dough. Sprinkle sugar then cinnamon evenly over top. Starting with widest end, roll dough into a tight log. Cut into 15 rolls; set aside.

Pour ½ cup melted butter into the bottom of a 9 x 13-inch pan. Sprinkle brown sugar evenly over butter. Sprinkle nuts over top. Place rolls cut side down in pan. Let dough rise for about 25 minutes.

Preheat oven to 350 degrees. When heated, bake rolls for 19–23 minutes. Invert hot rolls onto a platter.

Blueberry Applesauce Muffins

Makes **24** *muffins*

1 white cake mix
1 small box instant
   cheesecake or vanilla
   pudding
3/4 cup water
3 eggs, beaten
1/2 cup applesauce
1 (15-ounce) can
   blueberries, rinsed
   and drained

Preheat oven to 350 degrees.

Lightly grease and flour cups of a muffin pan or use paper liners and set aside.

In a bowl, mix together the cake mix, pudding mix, water, eggs, and applesauce until smooth. Gently fold in the blueberries. Fill muffin cups about 3/4 full. Bake for 19–25 minutes, or until light golden brown on top.

Oatmeal Raisin Muffins

Makes 24 *muffins*

1 yellow cake mix
1⅓ cups water
⅓ cup vegetable oil
2 large eggs
2 cups quick oats
1 cup raisins
½ cup chopped nuts
1½ teaspoons cinnamon

Preheat oven to 350 degrees.

Lightly grease and flour cups of a muffin pan or use paper liners and set aside.

In a bowl, mix together the cake mix, water, oil, eggs, and oats. Stir in raisins, nuts, and cinnamon. Fill muffin cups about ¾ full. Bake for 20–25 minutes, or until light golden brown on top.

Banana Nut Muffins

Makes 24 *muffins*

1 banana or spice
   cake mix
2 eggs
1 cup water
½ cup chopped nuts
⅓ cup vegetable oil
1 medium banana,
   mashed

Preheat oven to 350 degrees.

Lightly grease and flour cups of a muffin pan or use paper liners and set aside.

In a bowl, mix together the cake mix, eggs, water, nuts, oil, and banana until well blended. Fill muffin cups about ¾ full. Bake for 20–25 minutes, or until light golden brown on top.

Triple Chocolate Muffins

Makes **24** *muffins*

Preheat oven to 350 degrees.

1 chocolate fudge cake mix
1 small box instant chocolate pudding
¾ cup water
3 eggs, beaten
¼ cup applesauce
¼ cup vegetable oil
¼ teaspoon almond extract
¾ cup chocolate chips

Lightly grease and flour cups of a muffin pan or use paper liners and set aside.

In a bowl, mix together the cake mix, pudding mix, water, eggs, applesauce, oil, and almond extract until smooth. Stir in chocolate chips. Fill cups about ¾ full. Bake for 23–30 minutes, or until a toothpick inserted into the center comes out clean.

Sweet Banana Chocolate Chip Bread

Makes 2 loaves

2 medium bananas,
   mashed
1 banana or spice
   cake mix
1 small box instant
   banana pudding
3 eggs
1/4 cup vegetable oil
1/4 cup applesauce
3/4 teaspoon cinnamon
1/2 cup water

3/4 cup chocolate chips
Preheat oven to 350 degrees.

In a bowl, mix together all ingredients until smooth. Divide batter between two greased bread pans. Bake for 30 minutes, or until a toothpick inserted into the center comes out clean.

Basic Banana Bread

1 spice cake mix
3 large bananas, mashed
3 eggs
½ cup finely chopped nuts or raisins (optional)

Preheat oven to 350 degrees.

In a bowl, mix together all of the ingredients until smooth. Divide batter between two greased bread pans. Bake for 30 minutes, or until a toothpick inserted into the center comes out clean.

Easy Sweet Corn Bread

Makes 35 *servings*

2 boxes (8.5 ounces each) corn bread mix
1 yellow cake mix
Ingredients called for on back of each box

Preheat oven to 350 degrees.

Mix together all three boxes according to package directions. Combine the batters and then pour into a greased jelly roll pan or cookie sheet with sides. Bake for about 20–25 minutes, or until a toothpick inserted into the center comes out clean.

Brunch Crumb Cake

Makes **20** *servings*

1 yellow cake mix
Ingredients called for
   on back of box
1/2 cup sugar
1/2 cup firmly packed
   brown sugar
1 1/2 tablespoons
   cinnamon
2 cups flour
3/4 cup butter or
   margarine, melted

Preheat oven to 350 degrees.

Make cake batter as directed on back of box. Pour into a lightly greased and floured jelly roll pan or cookie sheet with sides. Bake for 15 minutes. Remove cake from oven and set aside.

In a bowl, mix together all of the remaining ingredients until crumbly. Sprinkle over cake. Bake for 10–15 minutes more, or until done.

Classic Coffee Cake

1 cup milk
1 (0.25-ounce) envelope
   or 2¼ teaspoons
   active dry yeast
1 yellow or white
   cake mix
3 eggs
½ cup vegetable oil
½ cup applesauce
¾ cup firmly packed
   brown sugar
½ cup flour
¼ cup butter or
   margarine, softened

Preheat oven to 350 degrees.

Warm milk in the microwave for about 35–45 seconds. Mix yeast with warm milk. Stir in cake mix, eggs, oil, and applesauce. Let stand in a draft free place for 5–10 minutes. Pour into a greased 9 x 13-inch pan and set aside.

In separate bowl, mix together the brown sugar, flour, and butter until crumbly. Sprinkle topping over batter. Bake for 25–32 minutes, or until a toothpick inserted into the center comes out clean.

Apple Nut Coffee Cake

Makes 15 *servings*

1 yellow cake mix,
    divided
1 cup flour
1 (0.25-ounce) envelope
    or 2¼ teaspoons
    active dry yeast
²/₃ cup warm water
2 large eggs
1 (21-ounce) can
    apple pie filling
½ cup chopped nuts
⅓ cup butter or
    margarine
1 cup powdered sugar
1 tablespoon milk

Preheat oven to 350 degrees.

In a bowl, mix together 1½ cups cake mix, flour, and yeast. Add warm water, stirring until smooth. Stir in eggs. Pour batter into a greased 9 x 13-inch pan. Spoon pie filling evenly over batter and then sprinkle nuts over top.

In a separate bowl, cut butter into remaining cake mix with a fork until crumbly. Sprinkle over top. Bake for 25–30 minutes, or until light golden brown; let cool.

In a bowl, combine the powdered sugar and milk. Drizzle over cake.

Cherry Coffee Cake

Makes 15 *servings*

1 yellow cake mix,
    divided
1 cup flour
1 (0.25-ounce) envelope
    or 2¼ teaspoons
    active dry yeast
²/₃ cup warm water
2 large eggs
1 (21-ounce) can
    cherry pie filling
½–²/₃ cup chopped
    chocolate (optional)
⅓ cup butter or
    margarine
1 cup sifted powdered
    sugar
1 tablespoon milk

Preheat oven to 350 degrees.

In a bowl, mix together 1½ cups cake mix, flour, and yeast. Add warm water, stirring until smooth. Stir in eggs. Pour batter into a greased 9 x 13-inch pan. Spoon pie filling evenly over top. Sprinkle with chocolate, if desired.

In a separate bowl, cut butter into remaining cake mix with a fork until crumbly. Sprinkle over top. Bake for 25–30 minutes, or until light golden brown; let cool.

In a bowl, combine the powdered sugar and milk. Drizzle over cake.

Cookies

Butter Pecan Cookies

Makes 36 cookies

Preheat oven to 350 degrees.

1 yellow or white
   cake mix
2 eggs
½ cup butter or
   margarine, melted
1 container coconut
   pecan frosting

In a bowl, use a spoon to mix together the cake mix, eggs, butter, and frosting. Refrigerate dough for 2 hours. Drop 1-inch dough balls onto a lightly greased cookie sheet. Bake for 10–11 minutes, or until light golden brown around edges. Remove cookies and place on a nonstick rack to cool.

Banana Nut Cookies

Makes 42 cookies

Preheat oven to 350 degrees.

1 white, yellow, or
   spice cake mix
2 eggs
⅓ cup butter or
   margarine, melted
⅓ cup applesauce
1 large banana, mashed
¾ cup chopped walnuts
   or pecans

In a bowl, use a spoon to mix together the cake mix, eggs, butter, and applesauce. Stir in the banana and nuts. Drop 1-inch dough balls onto a lightly greased cookie sheet. Bake for 9–12 minutes, or until light golden brown around edges. Remove cookies and place on a nonstick rack to cool.

Butterscotch Pecan Cookies

Makes 36 cookies

1 yellow or white
  cake mix
1 small box instant
  butterscotch pudding
½ cup flour
2 eggs
½ cup vegetable oil or
  melted butter
1 cup chopped pecans

Preheat oven to 350 degrees.

In a bowl, use a spoon to mix together the cake mix, pudding mix, flour, eggs, and oil. Stir in pecans. Drop 1-inch dough balls onto an ungreased cookie sheet. Bake for 9–12 minutes, or until light golden brown around edges. Remove cookies and place on a nonstick rack to cool.

Chocolate Peanut Butter Cookies

Makes 36 cookies

1 chocolate cake mix
2 eggs
½ cup vegetable oil or melted butter
1 cup peanut butter chips

Preheat oven to 350 degrees.

In a bowl, use a spoon to mix together the cake mix, eggs, and oil. Stir in peanut butter chips. Drop 1-inch dough balls onto an ungreased cookie sheet. Bake for 9–12 minutes, or until light golden brown around edges. Remove cookies and place on a nonstick rack to cool.

Chocolate Chip Crunch Cookies

2/3 cup butter-flavored
    shortening
1/2 cup firmly packed
    brown sugar
2 eggs
1 yellow or white
    cake mix
1 cup crispy rice cereal
1 cup semisweet or milk
    chocolate chips
1/2 cup chopped walnuts
    or pecans

Preheat oven to 350 degrees.

With a fork, blend together the shortening and brown sugar. Stir in eggs one at a time. Use a spoon to mix in the cake mix. Stir in the cereal, chocolate chips, and nuts. Drop 1-inch dough balls onto a lightly greased cookie sheet. Bake for 9–12 minutes, or until light golden brown around edges. Do not overbake. Cool for 2–3 minutes on pan. Remove cookies and place on a nonstick rack to cool.

Coconut Oatmeal Chocolate Chip Cookies

Makes 42 cookies

1 yellow or white
   cake mix
2 eggs
½ cup butter or
   margarine, softened
½ cup coconut
1½ cups quick oats
1 cup semisweet or milk
   chocolate chips

Preheat oven to 350 degrees.

In a bowl, use a spoon to mix together the cake mix, eggs, and butter. Stir in the coconut, oats, and chocolate chips. Drop 1-inch dough balls onto a lightly greased cookie sheet. Bake for 9–12 minutes, or until light golden brown around edges. Remove cookies and place on a nonstick rack to cool.

Moist Oatmeal Raisin Cookies

Makes 42 cookies

1 spice cake mix
2 eggs
1/3 cup vegetable oil
1/3 cup applesauce
2 cups quick oats
1 cup raisins

Preheat oven to 350 degrees.

In a bowl, use a spoon to mix together the cake mix, eggs, oil, and applesauce. Stir in the oats and raisins. Drop 1-inch dough balls onto a lightly greased cookie sheet. Bake for 9–12 minutes, or until light golden brown around edges. Remove cookies and place on a nonstick rack to cool.

Oatmeal Butterscotch Chip Cookies

Makes **42** *cookies*

**1 yellow or spice
   cake mix**
2 eggs
1/3 cup vegetable oil
1/3 cup applesauce
2 cups quick oats
1 cup butterscotch chips

Preheat oven to 350 degrees.

In a bowl, use a spoon to mix together the cake mix, eggs, oil, and applesauce. Stir in oats 1 cup at a time. Add butterscotch chips. Drop 1-inch dough balls onto a lightly greased cookie sheet. Bake for 9–12 minutes, or until light golden brown around edges. Remove cookies and place on a nonstick rack to cool.

Cherry Chip Sandwich Cookies

Makes 16–18
sandwich cookies

1 cherry chip cake mix
2 eggs
¹/₃ cup vegetable oil
1 container cherry or
vanilla frosting

Preheat oven to 350 degrees.

In a bowl, use a spoon to mix together the cake mix, eggs, and oil. Drop 1-inch dough balls onto a greased cookie sheet. Bake for 8–11 minutes, or until light golden brown around edges. Remove cookies and place on a nonstick rack to cool.

Spread frosting between 2 cooled cookies to form a sandwich.

NOTE: Ice cream sandwiches can be made using this recipe by replacing frosting with a scoop of vanilla ice cream. Just wrap sandwiches in plastic wrap and store in an airtight container in the freezer!

White Chocolate Lemon Cookies

Makes 32–36 cookies

1 lemon cake mix
2 eggs
⅓ cup vegetable oil
1 cup white chocolate
   chips

Preheat oven to 350 degrees.

In a bowl, use a spoon to mix together the cake mix, eggs, and oil. Stir in the white chocolate chips. Drop 1-inch dough balls onto a lightly greased cookie sheet. Bake for 8–12 minutes, or until light golden brown around edges. Remove cookies and place on a nonstick rack to cool.

NOTE: You can use this recipe to make bars in a 9 x 13-inch pan. Spread dough evenly into a lightly greased pan. Bake for 14–16 minutes, or until light golden brown around edges. Cool, then cut into bars.

Strawberry and Cream Cookies

Makes 30-32 *cookies*

1 strawberry cake mix
2 eggs
2 cups whipped topping
Powdered sugar

In a bowl, use a spoon to mix together the cake mix, eggs, and whipped topping; refrigerate for 2 hours.

Preheat oven to 350 degrees.

Roll 1-inch dough balls in the powdered sugar. Drop dough balls onto a greased cookie sheet. Bake for 6–9 minutes, or until light golden brown around edges. Remove cookies and place on a nonstick rack to cool. Store in refrigerator.

Peanut Butter–Chocolate Chip Cookies

Makes 32-36 cookies

2 eggs
1/3 cup butter or margarine, softened
1/2 cup peanut butter, creamy or chunky
1 yellow or white cake mix
1 cup chocolate chips or chunks

Preheat oven to 350 degrees.

In a bowl, use a spoon to mix together the eggs, butter, and peanut butter. Stir in cake mix until combined. Add chocolate chips or chunks. Drop 1-inch dough balls onto a lightly greased cookie sheet. Bake for 8–12 minutes, or until light golden brown around edges. Remove cookies and place on a nonstick rack to cool.

Fresh Orange Cookies

Makes 36 cookies

1 white cake mix
2 eggs
1/4 cup vegetable oil
1 cup flour
1/3 cup orange juice
1 tablespoon finely
 grated orange peel

Frosting
2 tablespoons butter or
 margarine, melted
1 1/2 cups powdered sugar
1 1/2 teaspoons finely
 grated orange peel
1–1 1/2 tablespoons
 orange juice

Preheat oven to 350 degrees.

In a bowl, use a spoon to mix together the cake mix, eggs, oil, flour, and orange juice. Stir in orange peel. Drop 1-inch dough balls onto a lightly greased cookie sheet. Bake for 10–13 minutes, or until light golden brown around edges. Remove cookies and place on a nonstick rack to cool.

In a separate bowl, mix together all of the frosting ingredients until smooth. Frost individual cookies as desired.

Peanut Butter Sandwich Cookies

Makes 16–18
sandwich cookies

2 eggs
**⅓ cup butter or
    margarine, softened**
**½ cup peanut butter,
    creamy or chunky**
**1 yellow or white
    cake mix**

Frosting
**¼ cup butter or
    margarine, melted**
3 cups powdered sugar
1 teaspoon vanilla
2 tablespoons water

Preheat oven to 350 degrees.

In a bowl, use a spoon to mix together the eggs, butter, and peanut butter. Stir in cake mix until well combined. Drop 1-inch dough balls onto a lightly greased cookie sheet. Bake for 8–12 minutes or until light golden brown around edges. Remove cookies and place on a nonstick rack to cool.

In a separate bowl, mix together all of the frosting ingredients until smooth. Spread frosting between 2 cooled cookies to form a sandwich.

NOTE: Ice cream sandwiches can be made using this recipe by replacing frosting with a scoop of vanilla or chocolate ice cream.

Pumpkin Chocolate Chip Cookies

Makes 5 dozen

2 packages yellow or
    spice cake mix
1 (29-ounce) can
    pumpkin
2 cups milk chocolate
    chips*

Preheat oven to 350 degrees.

In a bowl, use a spoon to mix together the cake mixes and pumpkin. Stir in chocolate chips. Drop by rounded spoonfuls onto a lightly greased cookie sheet. Bake for 8–12 minutes. Cool for 2–3 minutes on pan. Remove cookies and place on a nonstick rack to cool.

NOTE: Do not double this recipe.

*Butterscotch chips can be substituted.

Spiced Pumpkin Nut Cookies

Makes 30-36 cookies

1 spice cake mix
1 (15-ounce) can
    pumpkin
½ cup chopped nuts
1 cup milk chocolate
    chips or raisins
    (optional)

Preheat oven to 350 degrees.

In a bowl, use a spoon to mix together the cake mix and pumpkin. Stir in nuts and, if desired, chocolate chips or raisins. Drop by rounded spoonfuls onto a lightly greased cookie sheet. Bake for 8–12 minutes. Cool for 2–3 minutes on pan. Remove cookies and place on a nonstick rack to cool.

White Chocolate Chunk Cookies

Makes 36-42 cookies

Preheat oven to 350 degrees.

1 white cake mix
2 eggs
1/2 cup butter or
   margarine, softened
1 cup quick oats
1/2 cup chopped pecans
3/4 cup coconut
1 cup white chocolate
   chunks or chips

In a bowl, use a spoon to mix together the cake mix, eggs, and butter. Stir in oats, pecans, coconut, and white chocolate. Drop 1-inch dough balls onto an ungreased cookie sheet. Bake for 8–12 minutes, or until light golden brown around edges. Remove cookies and place on a nonstick rack to cool.

White Chocolate Macadamia Nut Cookies

Makes 32-36 cookies

1 white or yellow
   cake mix
2 eggs
1/3 cup vegetable oil
1 cup white chocolate
   chips or chunks
1/2 cup chopped
   macadamia nuts

Preheat oven to 350 degrees.

In a bowl, use a spoon to mix together the cake mix, eggs, and oil. Stir in white chocolate and nuts. Drop 1-inch dough balls onto an ungreased cookie sheet. Bake for 8–12 minutes, or until light golden brown around edges. Remove cookies and place on a nonstick rack to cool.

NOTE: Try substituting milk chocolate or semisweet chips in place of the white chocolate.

Chocolate Mint Surprise Cookies

Makes 32-36 cookies

1 chocolate cake mix
2 eggs
½ cup vegetable oil
30–36 individual Andes mints, unwrapped

Preheat oven to 350 degrees.

In a bowl, use a spoon to mix together the cake mix, eggs, and oil. Flatten a 1-inch ball of dough and then wrap around a mint. Make sure candy is completely covered with dough. Bake for 8–12 minutes. Remove cookies and place on a nonstick rack to cool.

Peanut Butter Cup Cookies

Makes 32-36 cookies

1 chocolate cake mix
2 eggs
⅓ cup vegetable oil
1 bag miniature Reese's Peanut Butter Cups

Preheat oven to 350 degrees.

In a bowl, use a spoon to mix together the cake mix, eggs, and oil. Flatten a 1-inch ball of dough and then wrap around a peanut butter cup. Make sure candy is completely covered with dough. Bake for 8–12 minutes, or until done. Remove cookies and place on a nonstick rack to cool.

Chewy Lemon Cookies

Makes 30-32 cookies

1 lemon cake mix
2 eggs
2 cups whipped topping
Powdered sugar
**1 container cream
cheese frosting**
**2 teaspoons grated
lemon rind (optional)**

In a bowl, use a spoon to mix together the cake mix, eggs, and whipped topping; refrigerate for 2 hours.

Preheat oven to 350 degrees.

Roll 1-inch dough balls in the powdered sugar. Drop dough balls onto a greased cookie sheet. Bake for 6–9 minutes, or until light golden brown around edges. Remove cookies and place on a nonstick rack to cool.

Mix together the frosting and lemon rind, if desired. Top cooled cookies with frosting. Store in refrigerator.

Sweet Honey Cookies

Makes 32-36 cookies

1 cake mix, any
    flavor, divided
2 eggs
⅓ cup honey
⅓ cup butter or
    margarine
½ cup flour

Preheat oven to 350 degrees.

In a bowl, use a spoon to mix together half of the cake mix with the eggs, honey, butter, and flour, beating until fluffy. Stir in the remaining cake mix until absorbed. Drop rounded spoonfuls of dough onto an ungreased cookie sheet. Bake for 10–12 minutes, or until light golden brown around edges. Remove cookies and place on a nonstick rack to cool.

Chocolate Chip Delights

Makes 32-36 cookies

Preheat oven to 350 degrees.

1 cake mix, any flavor
¼ cup light brown sugar
⅓ cup oil
2 eggs
¾ cup chocolate chips

In a bowl, use a spoon to mix together the cake mix, brown sugar, oil, and eggs. Stir in chocolate chips. Drop 1-inch dough balls onto greased cookie sheet. Bake for 10–12 minutes, or until light golden brown around edges. Remove cookies and place on a nonstick rack to cool.

Nutty Chocolate Chip Cookies

Makes 36 cookies

1 yellow cake mix, divided
1/2 cup butter or margarine, softened
1 teaspoon vanilla
2 eggs
2/3 cup chocolate chips
1/2 cup chopped nuts

Preheat oven to 350 degrees.

In a bowl, use a spoon to mix together half of the cake mix with the butter, vanilla, and eggs until smooth. Stir in chocolate chips and nuts. Stir in the remaining cake mix until absorbed. Drop rounded spoonfuls of dough onto an ungreased cookie sheet. Bake for 10–12 minutes, or until light golden brown around edges. Remove cookies and place on a nonstick rack to cool.

Peanut Butter–Chocolate Kiss Cookies

Makes 32-36 *cookies*

Preheat oven to 350 degrees.

1 yellow cake mix
2 eggs
1/3 cup oil
3/4 cup peanut butter, creamy or crunchy
1 bag Hershey's Kisses

In a bowl, use a spoon to mix together the cake mix, eggs, and oil. Stir in the peanut butter. Drop 1-inch dough balls onto a lightly greased pan. Press an unwrapped chocolate in the center of each dough ball. Bake for 10 minutes, or until light golden brown around edges. Remove cookies and place on a nonstick rack to cool.

Easy Snickerdoodles

Makes 32–36 cookies

1 yellow cake mix
1 teaspoon vanilla
    extract
1/3 cup vegetable oil
2 eggs
1/2 cup sugar mixed
    with 2 teaspoons
    cinnamon

Preheat oven to 375 degrees.

In a bowl, use a spoon to mix together the cake mix, vanilla, oil, and eggs. Roll dough into 1-inch balls and then roll in the sugar mixture. Bake for 8–10 minutes, or until light golden brown around the edges. Remove cookies and place on a nonstick rack to cool.

Butterfinger Cookies

Makes 32–36 cookies

1 yellow or chocolate
    cake mix
2 eggs
1/3 cup vegetable oil
1 king-size Butterfinger
    candy bar

Preheat oven to 350 degrees.

In a bowl, use a spoon to mix together the cake mix, eggs, and oil. Chop Butterfinger into tiny pieces and then mix into the dough. Drop 1-inch dough balls onto a greased cookie sheet. Bake for 10–12 minutes, or until light golden brown around edges. Remove cookies and place on a nonstick rack to cool.

Quick and Easy Peanut Butter Cookies

Makes 32-36 cookies

1 yellow cake mix
2 eggs
1/3 cup oil
3/4 cup peanut butter,
    crunchy or creamy
Sugar

Preheat oven to 350 degrees.

In a bowl, use a spoon to mix together the cake mix, eggs, and oil. Stir in the peanut butter. Drop 1-inch dough balls into a small bowl of sugar and then place on a greased cookie sheet. Press fork horizontally and then vertically across the top of each ball to flatten. Bake for 10–12 minutes, or until light golden brown around edges. Remove cookies and place on a nonstick rack to cool.

Chocolate Butterscotch Cookies

Makes 32-36 cookies

Preheat oven to 350 degrees.

1 chocolate cake mix
2 eggs
1/3 cup vegetable oil
1 cup butterscotch chips

In a bowl, use a spoon to mix together the cake mix, eggs, and oil. Stir in butterscotch chips. Drop 1-inch dough balls onto a greased cookie sheet. Bake for 9–12 minutes, or until light golden brown around edges. Remove cookies and place on a nonstick rack to cool.

Easy M&M Cookies

Makes 32-36 cookies

Preheat oven to 350 degrees.

1 white cake mix
2 eggs
1/3 cup vegetable oil
1¼ cups plain M&Ms

In a bowl, use a spoon to mix together the cake mix, eggs, and oil. Stir in the M&Ms. Drop 1-inch dough balls onto greased cookie sheet. Bake for 9–12 minutes, or until light golden brown around edges. Remove cookies and place on a nonstick rack to cool.

Chewy Oreo Cookies

Makes 16–18
sandwich cookies

1 chocolate cake mix
2 eggs
2 cups whipped topping
Powdered sugar
1 container vanilla
   or cream cheese
   frosting

In a bowl, use a spoon to mix together the cake mix, eggs, and whipped topping; refrigerate for 2 hours.

Preheat oven to 350 degrees.

Roll dough into 1-inch balls and then roll in the powdered sugar. Place on a lightly greased cookie sheet. Bake for 7–10 minutes. Remove cookies and place on a nonstick rack to cool.

Spread frosting between 2 cookies to form a sandwich.

Snickers Surprise Cookies

Makes 32-36 cookies

1 yellow or chocolate cake mix
2 eggs
$1/3$ cup vegetable oil
1 bag Snickers Miniatures

Preheat oven to 350 degrees.

In a bowl, use a spoon to mix together the cake mix, eggs, and oil. Flatten 1-inch dough balls and wrap around a candy. Make sure candy is completely covered with dough. Bake for 8–10 minutes. Remove cookies and place on a nonstick rack to cool.

Brownies & Bars

Caramel Cashew Bars

Makes 18–20 *servings*

1 yellow or white
    cake mix
2 eggs
1/3 cup vegetable oil or
    melted butter
1 cup chopped cashews
1 cup semisweet or milk
    chocolate chips
25 caramels, unwrapped
1/8 cup milk

Preheat oven to 350 degrees.

In a bowl, use a spoon to mix together the cake mix, eggs, and oil. Stir in cashews and chocolate chips. Press dough evenly into a lightly greased 9 x 13-inch pan. Bake for 16–20 minutes, or until light golden brown around edges.

In a saucepan, heat together the caramels and milk, stirring constantly, until the caramels are melted. Pour caramel topping evenly over baked dessert. Cool completely and cut into bars.

Caramel Chocolate Chip Bars

Makes 18–20 *servings*

1 yellow cake mix
1/2 cup butter or
   margarine, melted
1/4 cup evaporated milk
1 cup chocolate chips
3/4 cup chopped nuts
1 (12-ounce) jar caramel
   ice cream topping

Preheat oven to 350 degrees.

In a bowl, use a spoon to mix together the cake mix, butter, and milk. Press 3/4 of the dough evenly into a greased 9 x 13-inch pan. Sprinkle chocolate chips and nuts over the dough. Pour the caramel topping evenly over chocolate chip layer. Break rest of dough into small pieces and then evenly drop over top. Bake for 20–25 minutes; cool at least 30 minutes. Cut into bars. Store in refrigerator.

Chocolate Chip Toffee Bars

Makes 18–20 *servings*

1 yellow or white
   cake mix
2 eggs
1/3 cup vegetable oil
   or melted butter
1/2 cup Skor toffee
   bits or crushed
   Heath bars
1/2 cup chocolate chips

Preheat oven to 350 degrees.

In a bowl, use a spoon to mix together the cake mix, eggs, and oil. Stir in the toffee and chocolate chips. Press dough evenly into a lightly greased 9 x 13-inch pan. Bake for 14–20 minutes, or until light golden brown around edges. Cut into bars and serve warm or at room temperature.

NOTE: Crushed Butterfinger bars may be used in place of the toffee bits.

Peanut Butter Layer Bars

Makes **18–20** *servings*

1 yellow or white
   cake mix
1/2 cup butter or
   margarine, melted
1 egg
1/2 cup creamy peanut
   butter
1 cup chocolate chips
1 cup peanut butter
   chips
3/4 cup chopped nuts
   (optional)
1 (14-ounce) can sweet-
   ened condensed milk

Preheat oven to 350 degrees.

In a bowl, use a spoon to mix together the cake mix, butter, egg, and peanut butter. Press dough into a lightly greased 9 x 13-inch pan. Sprinkle chocolate chips, peanut butter chips, and nuts, if desired, over dough. Pour sweetened condensed milk evenly over top. Bake for 20–25 minutes, or until light golden brown around edges. Cool completely and cut into bars.

Coconut Cream Cheese Blondies

Makes 18–20 *servings*

1 white cake mix
1/2 cup butter or
   margarine, melted
3 eggs, divided
3/4 cup chopped pecans
3/4 cup coconut
1 (8-ounce) package
   cream cheese,
   softened
1/2 teaspoon vanilla
1 pound powdered sugar

Preheat oven to 350 degrees.

In a bowl, use a spoon to mix together the mix cake mix, butter, and 1 egg. Press dough into a lightly greased 9 x 13-inch pan. Sprinkle pecans and coconut evenly over top.

In a separate bowl, use an electric mixer to gradually beat together the cream cheese, vanilla, and remaining eggs. Slowly beat in the powdered sugar. Spread cream cheese mixture evenly over pecan and coconut layer. Bake for 30–35 minutes, or until light golden brown around edges. Store in refrigerator.

Cookie Dough Blondies

Makes 18–20 *servings*

1 yellow or white
    cake mix
1 cup butter or
    margarine,
    softened, divided
1 egg
2 teaspoons vanilla,
    divided
¾ cup firmly packed
    brown sugar, divided
¾ cup semisweet
    chocolate chips
¼ cup sugar
2 tablespoons milk
1 cup flour

Frosting
1 tablespoon butter or
    margarine
1 cup semisweet
    chocolate chips

Preheat oven to 350 degrees.

In a bowl, use a spoon to mix together the cake mix, ½ cup butter, egg, 1 teaspoon vanilla, and ¼ cup brown sugar. Stir in the chocolate chips. Press evenly into a greased 9 x 13-inch pan. Bake for 15–20 minutes, or until light golden brown around edges; cool completely.

In a separate bowl, mix together the remaining butter and sugars. Stir in the milk and remaining vanilla, followed by the flour. Spread evenly over cooled bottom layer.

To make the frosting, melt together the butter and chocolate chips in a small saucepan until smooth. Spread melted chocolate over top. Refrigerate at least 2 hours before serving. Cut into bars. Store in refrigerator.

Peanut Butter Crunch Bars

Makes 18–20 servings

1 white or yellow
   cake mix
2 eggs
1/3 cup vegetable oil
1/2 cup creamy peanut
   butter

Topping
1 cup semisweet or milk
   chocolate chips
1/2 cup creamy peanut
   butter
1 1/2 cups crispy rice
   cereal

Preheat oven to 350 degrees.

In a bowl, use a spoon to mix together the cake mix, eggs, and oil. Stir in the peanut butter. Press dough evenly into a lightly greased 9 x 13-inch pan. Bake for 14–18 minutes, or until light golden brown around edges; set aside.

To make the topping, melt the chocolate chips and peanut butter over low heat. Remove from heat and fold in cereal. Spread mixture evenly over cooled bars. Cool completely and chill at least 2 hours. Cut into bars before serving. Store in refrigerator.

Chocolate–Peanut Butter Coconut Bars

Makes 18–20 *servings*

1 yellow cake mix
1/2 cup butter or
    margarine, melted
1 egg
1 1/2 cups coconut
1 (14-ounce) can sweet-
    ened condensed milk

Topping
1 1/2 cups semisweet or
    milk chocolate chips
1/3 cup creamy peanut
    butter

Preheat oven to 350 degrees.

In a bowl, use a spoon to mix together the cake mix, butter, and egg. Press dough into a lightly greased 9 x 13-inch glass pan. Sprinkle coconut over top. Pour condensed milk evenly over coconut. Bake for 20–25 minutes, or until light golden brown around edges.

In a saucepan over low heat, melt together the chocolate chips and peanut butter. Spread chocolate over hot coconut layer. Cool for 30 minutes. Chill for at least 2 hours. Store in refrigerator.

Peanut Butter M&M Bars

Makes 18–20 servings

Preheat oven to 350 degrees.

1 white or yellow
   cake mix
2 eggs
1/3 cup vegetable oil
1/2 cup peanut butter,
   chunky or creamy
1 1/2 cups M&Ms

In a bowl, use a spoon to mix together the cake mix, eggs, oil, and peanut butter. Mix M&Ms into the dough. Press dough into a lightly greased 9 x 13-inch pan. Bake for 14–18 minutes, or until light golden brown around edges. Cool for 15–20 minutes before cutting into bars.

Chocolate Mint Chip Bars

Makes 18–20 servings

Preheat oven to 350 degrees.

1 chocolate cake mix
2 eggs
1/2 cup vegetable oil
1 cup mint chips

In a bowl, use a spoon to mix together the cake mix, eggs, and oil. Stir in the mint chips. Press dough into a lightly greased 9 x 13-inch pan. Bake for 14–16 minutes. Cool, then cut into bars.

Six Layer Bars

1 yellow cake mix
½ cup butter or
    margarine, melted
1 egg
1 (14-ounce) can sweet-
    ened condensed milk
1 cup coconut
1 cup chocolate chips
1 cup butterscotch chips
¾ cup chopped nuts

Preheat oven to 350 degrees.

In a bowl, use a spoon to mix together the cake mix, butter, and egg. Press dough into a lightly greased 9 x 13-inch pan. Sprinkle coconut, chocolate chips, butterscotch chips, and nuts evenly over dough. Pour condensed milk over top. Bake for 20–25 minutes, or until light golden brown around edges. Cool completely and cut into bars.

White Chocolate and Fudge Brownies

Makes 18–20 servings

1 chocolate fudge
    cake mix
2 eggs
⅓ cup oil
¾ cup white chocolate
    chips

Preheat oven to 350 degrees.

In a bowl, use a spoon to mix together the cake mix, eggs, and oil. Stir in the white chocolate chips. Press dough into a greased 9 x 13-inch pan. Bake for 14–16 minutes. Serve warm or at room temperature. Can be topped with favorite frosting, if desired.

Strawberry Pudding Bars

Makes 18–20 servings

Preheat oven to 350 degrees.

1 strawberry cake mix
2 eggs
1/3 cup vegetable oil
1 cup white chocolate or
   vanilla chips
1 small box vanilla or
   cheesecake instant
   pudding
1½ cups milk

In a bowl, use a spoon to mix together the cake mix, eggs, and oil. Stir in the white chips. Press dough into a lightly greased 9 x 13-inch pan. Bake for 14–18 minutes, or until light golden brown around edges. Immediately poke holes in dessert at 1-inch intervals with a wooden spoon handle.

In a separate bowl, use a wire whisk to beat together the pudding mix and milk for 2 minutes. Pour half of the pudding mixture over the warm bars. Let remaining pudding chill and thicken, about 5–10 minutes. Frost with remaining pudding and cut into bars. Store in refrigerator.

Oatmeal–Caramel Apple Bars

Makes 18–20 *servings*

1 yellow, white, or
  spice cake mix
2 eggs
1/2 cup butter or
  margarine, softened
1 1/2 cups quick oats
2 cups peeled and
  chopped apples
1/2 cup chopped walnuts
  or pecans
1/2 cup flour
1 (16-ounce) jar caramel
  ice cream topping

Preheat oven to 350 degrees.

In a bowl, use a spoon to mix together the cake mix, eggs, and butter. Stir in the oats. Press dough into a greased 9 x 13-inch pan. Sprinkle apples and nuts evenly over dough. Bake for 25–30 minutes.

In a saucepan, heat together the flour and caramel topping, stirring constantly, and bring to boil. Continue stirring and boil 3–5 minutes to thicken. Remove from heat and drizzle over the apple layer; cool completely. Refrigerate for 1 hour and then cut into bars. Store in an airtight container in refrigerator.

Luscious Lemon Bars

Makes **18–20** servings

Preheat oven to 350 degrees.

1 white or yellow
    cake mix
½ cup butter or
    margarine, melted
1 egg
3 eggs, slightly beaten
1¾ cups sugar
¼ cup flour
1 teaspoon baking
    powder
¼ cup lemon juice
Powdered sugar

In a bowl, use a spoon to mix together the cake mix, butter, and 1 egg. Press dough into a greased 9 x 13-inch pan.

Mix together the slightly beaten eggs, sugar, flour, baking powder, and lemon juice. Spread evenly over the dough. Bake for 30–35 minutes, or until light golden brown on top; cool completely. Sprinkle powdered sugar over top and cut into bars. Store in refrigerator.

Pineapple Cream Cheese Bars

Makes 18–20 *servings*

1 white or yellow
   cake mix
1/2 cup butter or
   margarine, melted
1 egg
1 (8-ounce) package
   cream cheese,
   softened
2 tablespoons sugar
2 tablespoons milk
1 teaspoon vanilla
1 egg
1 (8-ounce) can crushed
   pineapple, drained
1–1½ cups coconut

Glaze
3/4 cup powdered sugar
1/4 teaspoon vanilla
3–4 teaspoons milk

Preheat oven to 350 degrees.

In a bowl, use a spoon to mix together the cake mix, butter, and egg. Press dough into a lightly greased 9 x 13-inch pan; set aside.

In a separate bowl, beat together the cream cheese, sugar, milk, vanilla, and egg until smooth. Stir in the well-drained pineapple. Spread mixture evenly over the dough. Sprinkle coconut over top. Bake for 25–30 minutes, or until coconut is light golden brown; cool completely.

In a bowl, mix together the glaze ingredients until smooth. Drizzle evenly over cooled dessert. Refrigerate at least 2 hours and cut into bars. Store in refrigerator.

Butter Pecan Bars

Makes 18–20 *servings*

1 butter pecan or
    white cake mix
2 eggs
1/3 cup butter or
    margarine, melted
1 teaspoon vanilla
1/2 cup chopped pecans
12–15 pecan halves
    (optional)

Frosting
2 tablespoons butter or
    margarine, melted
2 cups powdered sugar
1/4 teaspoon vanilla
2–3 tablespoons milk

Preheat oven to 350 degrees.

In a bowl, use a spoon to mix together the cake mix, eggs, butter, and vanilla. Stir in the chopped pecans. Press dough into a lightly greased 9 x 13-inch pan. Bake for 14–16 minutes, or until light golden brown around edges. Cool for 15–20 minutes.

In a separate bowl, mix together the frosting ingredients until smooth. Spread evenly over top of cooled dessert. Cut into bars. Place a pecan half in the center of each bar, if desired.

Easy Lemon Squares

Makes **18–20** servings

Preheat oven to 350 degrees.

1 lemon cake mix
2 eggs
⅓ cup oil
Powdered sugar

In a bowl, use a spoon to mix together the cake mix, eggs, and oil. Press dough into a greased 9 x 13-inch pan. Bake for 13–15 minutes, or until light golden brown on top. Cool and then sprinkle with powdered sugar.

Simplest Brownies

Makes **18–20** servings

Preheat oven to 350 degrees.

1 chocolate cake mix
2 eggs
½ cup oil

In a bowl, use a spoon to mix together the cake mix, eggs, and oil. Press dough into a greased 9 x 13-inch pan. Bake for 13–16 minutes, or until the desired consistency.

Peanut Butter–Chocolate Chip Bars

Makes **18–20** *servings*

1 chocolate chip or
    yellow cake mix
2 eggs
⅓ cup vegetable oil
½ cup peanut butter,
    chunky or creamy
1 cup chocolate chips

Preheat oven to 350 degrees.

In a bowl, use a spoon to mix together the cake mix, eggs, and oil. Mix in the peanut butter. Stir in the chocolate chips. Press dough into a lightly greased 9 x 13-inch pan. Bake for 14–17 minutes, or until golden brown. When cooled, cut into bars and serve.

Nutty Chocolate Chip Brownies

Makes 18–20 *servings*

1 chocolate cake mix
1/2 cup butter or
    margarine, softened
3 eggs
3/4 cup semisweet
    chocolate chips
1/2 cup chopped nuts

Preheat oven to 350 degrees.

In a bowl, use a spoon to mix together the cake mix, butter, and eggs. Stir in chocolate chips and nuts. Press dough into a greased 9 x 13-inch pan. Bake for 26–30 minutes. When cooled, cut into squares and serve.

Easy Cherry Chip Squares

Makes 18–20 *servings*

1 cherry chip cake mix
2 eggs
1/3 cup oil

Preheat oven to 350 degrees.

In a bowl, use a spoon to mix together the cake mix, eggs, and oil. Press dough into a greased 9 x 13-inch pan. Bake for 13–17 minutes, or until light golden brown on top. Serve warm or at room temperature.

Lemon Cream Cheese Bars

Makes 18–20 servings

1 lemon cake mix
1 egg
1/2 cup butter or
    margarine, melted
3 3/4 cups powdered sugar
2 eggs, beaten
1 (8-ounce) package
    cream cheese, softened
1 teaspoon vanilla

Preheat oven to 350 degrees.

In a bowl, use a spoon to mix together the cake mix, egg, and butter. Press dough into a greased 9 x 13-inch pan.

In a separate bowl, beat together the powdered sugar, eggs, cream cheese, and vanilla until smooth. Spread mixture over dough. Bake for 30–35 minutes, or until top turns a light golden brown.

Chewy Strawberry Squares

Makes **18–20** *servings*

1 strawberry cake mix
2 eggs
1/3 cup oil
1 1/2 tablespoons milk
1 cup powdered sugar

Preheat oven to 350 degrees.

In a bowl, use a spoon to mix together the cake mix, eggs, and oil. Press dough into a 9 x 13-inch pan. Bake for 14–16 minutes.

In a bowl, whisk together the milk and powdered sugar. Drizzle over the squares while still warm. Serve warm or at room temperature.

Chewy Chocolate Chip Bars

Makes **18–20** *servings*

1 yellow or white
   cake mix
2 eggs
1/3 cup oil
3/4 cup chocolate chips

Preheat oven to 350 degrees.

In a bowl, use a spoon to mix together the cake mix, eggs, and oil. Stir in chocolate chips. Press dough into a 9 x 13-inch pan. Bake for 14–16 minutes, or until light golden brown on top. Serve warm or at room temperature.

Peanut Butter Brownies

Makes 18–20 *servings*

1 yellow or white
   cake mix
1/3 cup oil
2 eggs
2/3 cup peanut butter,
   chunky or creamy
1 cup powdered sugar
1 1/2 tablespoons milk

Preheat oven to 350 degrees.

In a bowl, use a spoon to mix together the cake mix, oil, and eggs. Stir in the peanut butter. Press dough into a lightly greased 9 x 13-inch pan. Bake for 14–16 minutes, or until golden brown on top.

In a bowl, whisk together the powdered sugar and milk. Drizzle over brownies while still warm. Serve warm or at room temperature.

Cream Cheese Brownies

Makes 18–20 servings

1 chocolate cake mix
1/2 cup butter or
   margarine, melted
3 eggs, divided
1/2 cup chopped pecans
   (optional)
1 pound powdered sugar
1 (8-ounce) package
   cream cheese

Preheat oven to 350 degrees.

In a bowl, use a spoon to mix together the cake mix, butter, and 1 egg. Add pecans, if desired. Press dough into a greased 9 x 13-inch pan.

In a separate bowl, beat together the powdered sugar, cream cheese, and remaining eggs; spread over dough. Bake for 35–40 minutes, or until golden brown.

Apple Cinnamon Bars

Makes 18–20 servings

½ cup butter or
    margarine, softened
1 yellow cake mix
⅓ cup coconut
4 medium apples,
    peeled, cored, and
    thinly sliced
½ cup sugar
1 teaspoon cinnamon
1 cup sour cream
1 egg, beaten

Preheat oven to 350 degrees.

In a bowl, use a fork or pastry blender to cut butter into cake mix until crumbly. Stir in coconut. Press mixture into an ungreased 9 x 13-inch pan. Pat slightly up on the sides of the pan as well. Bake for 10 minutes.

Arrange apple slices on the warm crust. Mix together the sugar and cinnamon and then sprinkle over the apples. Blend the sour cream into the egg. Drizzle mixture over the top. Bake for 25 minutes, or until edges are lightly golden. Serve warm.

Butterscotch Nut Bars

1 yellow cake mix
2 eggs
⅓ cup oil
¾ cup butterscotch
   chips
½ cup chopped nuts

Preheat oven to 350 degrees.

In a bowl, use a spoon to mix together the cake mix, eggs, and oil. Stir in the butterscotch chips and nuts. Press dough into a lightly greased 9 x 13-inch pan. Bake for 13–16 minutes, or until light golden brown on top.

Reese's Peanut Butter Bars

Makes 18–20 *servings*

1 yellow cake mix
2 eggs
1/3 cup oil
1 cup Reese's Pieces
3/4 cup chopped Reese's
   Peanut Butter Cups

Preheat oven to 350 degrees.

In a bowl, use a spoon to mix together the cake mix, eggs, and oil. Stir in the candies. Press dough into a greased 9 x 13-inch pan. Bake for 13–17 minutes, or until golden brown.

Pumpkin Pie Bars

Makes 18–20 *servings*

1 (29-ounce) can
    pumpkin
1 cup milk
1 cup sugar
2 eggs
1 teaspoon cinnamon
1/2 teaspoon nutmeg
1/2 teaspoon ginger
1/2 teaspoon salt
1 yellow cake mix
3/4 cup chopped walnuts
3/4 cup butter or
    margarine, melted

Preheat oven to 350 degrees.

In a bowl, use a spoon to mix together the pumpkin, milk, sugar, eggs, spices, and salt. Spread mixture into a lightly greased 9 x 13-inch glass pan. Pat yellow cake mix over bottom layer. Spread walnuts over dry mix. Cover dry mix with melted butter. Bake for 45–55 minutes, or until golden brown on top.

Cream Cheese Bars

Makes 18–20 *servings*

1 yellow cake mix
1 egg
1/3 cup oil
1 (8–ounce) package
    cream cheese
1/3 cup sugar
1 teaspoon lemon juice
1 egg

Preheat oven to 350 degrees.

In a bowl, mix together the cake mix, egg, and oil until crumbly. Set aside 1 cup for topping. Press remaining dough lightly into a greased 9 x 13-inch pan. Bake for 15 minutes.

In a separate bowl, beat together the cream cheese, sugar, lemon juice, and egg until smooth. Spread evenly over baked layer. Sprinkle with reserved crust mixture. Bake for 15 minutes more. Cool and cut into bars.

German Chocolate Bars

Makes **18–20** *servings*

1 German chocolate
   cake mix
1 cup quick oats
½ cup butter or
   margarine, softened
3 eggs, divided
1 (8-ounce) package
   cream cheese
1 container coconut
   pecan frosting

Preheat oven to 350 degrees.

In a bowl, use a fork to mix together the cake mix, oats, butter, and 1 egg until crumbly; reserve 2 cups. Press remaining dough into a greased 9 x 13-inch pan.

In a separate bowl, beat together the cream cheese and remaining eggs until smooth. Stir the frosting into the cream cheese mixture. Spread over crust. Sprinkle reserved crust mixture over the cream cheese layer. Bake for 33–38 minutes, or until done.

Peanut Butter Lush

Makes 15–18 servings

1 white or yellow
  cake mix
1/2 cup butter or
  margarine, melted
1 egg
2 small boxes instant
  chocolate pudding
3 1/4 cups cold milk,
  divided
1/3 cup creamy peanut
  butter
1 (12-ounce) container
  whipped topping
Nuts, to garnish
Chocolate syrup, to
  garnish

Preheat oven to 350 degrees.

In a bowl, use a spoon to mix together the cake mix, butter, and egg. Press dough into a lightly greased 9 x 13-inch pan. Bake for 14–18 minutes, or until light golden brown around edges. Using a spoon, remove air pockets by pushing down evenly over entire hot crust; cool completely.

In a separate bowl, use a wire whisk to beat the pudding mixes with 3 cups milk for 2 minutes. Spread evenly over cooled crust.

In another bowl, use a wire whisk to mix together the peanut butter, remaining milk, and whipped topping. Gently spread peanut butter mixture evenly over the pudding layer. Chill for 3–4 hours before serving. To garnish, sprinkle with nuts and drizzle chocolate syrup lightly over top before serving. Store in refrigerator.

Banana Cream Pie Bars

Makes 15–18 *servings*

1 white or yellow
  cake mix
1/2 cup butter or
  margarine, melted
1 egg
2 medium bananas,
  thinly sliced
2 small boxes instant
  banana pudding
3 cups cold milk
1 (12-ounce) container
  whipped topping

Preheat oven to 350 degrees.

In a bowl, use a spoon to mix together the cake mix, butter, and egg. Press dough into a lightly greased 9 x 13-inch pan. Bake for 14–18 minutes, or until light golden brown around edges. Using a spoon, remove air pockets by pushing down evenly over entire hot crust; cool completely.

Place banana slices evenly over the crust.

In a separate bowl, use a wire whisk to beat together the pudding mixes and milk for 2 minutes. Spread evenly over banana slices. Chill for 3–4 hours. Spread the whipped topping over top before serving. Store in refrigerator.

Cream Cheese Coconut Pudding Bars

Makes 15–18 servings

1 white or yellow
   cake mix
½ cup butter or
   margarine, melted
1 egg
1 (8–ounce) package
   cream cheese,
   softened
¼ cup sugar
3 cups plus 2 tablespoons
   milk, divided
1 (12-ounce) container
   whipped topping,
   divided
2 small boxes instant
   coconut cream
   pudding
½ cup coconut

Preheat oven to 350 degrees.

In a bowl, use a spoon to mix together the cake mix, butter, and egg. Press dough into a lightly greased 9 x 13-inch pan. Bake for 14–18 minutes, or until light golden brown around edges. Using a spoon, remove air pockets by pushing down evenly over entire hot crust; cool completely.

In a separate bowl, beat together the cream cheese, sugar, and 2 tablespoons milk. Gently stir in 1 cup whipped topping and then spread over the crust.

In another bowl, use a whisk to beat together the pudding mixes and remaining milk for 2 minutes. Spread over the cream cheese layer. Chill for 3–4 hours. Before serving, spread remaining whipped topping over the pudding layer and sprinkle coconut over top. Store in refrigerator.

Chilled Cherry Pineapple Bars

Makes 15–18 servings

1 white or yellow
  cake mix
1 egg
1/3–1/2 cup butter or
  margarine, melted
2 (21-ounce) cans
  cherry pie filling
1 (20-ounce) can
  crushed pineapple,
  drained
1 (12-ounce) container
  whipped topping
1 (14-ounce) can sweet-
  ened condensed milk
1 cup chopped pecans

Preheat oven to 350 degrees.

In a bowl, use a spoon to mix together the cake mix, egg, and butter. Press dough into a lightly greased 9 x 13-inch pan. Bake for 14–18 minutes, or until light golden brown around edges. Using a spoon, remove air pockets by pushing down evenly over entire hot crust; cool completely.

In a separate bowl, stir together the pie filling, pineapple, whipped topping, and condensed milk. Pour over the crust. Sprinkle pecans over top. Chill for at least 4 hours. Cut into bars and serve. Store in refrigerator.

Peaches-and-Cream Pudding Bars

Makes 15–18 servings

1 white or yellow
   cake mix
1 egg
1/3–1/2 cup butter or
   margarine, melted
2 small boxes instant
   vanilla or cheesecake
   pudding
3 cups milk
1 (29-ounce) can sliced
   peaches, drained
1 (12-ounce) container
   whipped topping
Fresh sliced peaches
   (optional)

Preheat oven to 350 degrees.

In a bowl, use a spoon to mix together the cake mix, egg, and butter. Press dough into a lightly greased 9 x 13-inch pan. Bake for 14–18 minutes, or until light golden brown around edges. Using a spoon, remove air pockets by pushing down evenly over entire hot crust; cool completely.

In a separate bowl, use a wire whisk to mix together the pudding mixes and milk until thick; chill for 5–10 minutes. Place half of the peaches evenly over the crust. Spread half of pudding over peaches. Place remaining peaches over pudding and then spread the remaining pudding over top. Cover and chill for least 3 hours. Before serving, spread the whipped topping over top and garnish with fresh peaches, if desired. Cut into bars and serve. Store in refrigerator.

Chewy Gooey Peanut Bars

Makes 15–18 *servings*

Preheat oven to 350 degrees.

1 white cake mix
1 egg
½ cup butter or
   margarine, melted
3½ cups miniature
   marshmallows
1¾ cups peanut butter
   chips
3 tablespoons butter or
   margarine
⅔ cup corn syrup
1 (16-ounce) can
   chopped peanuts

In a bowl, use a spoon to mix together the cake mix, egg, and ½ cup melted butter. Press dough into a lightly greased 9 x 13-inch pan. Bake for 15–18 minutes or until light golden brown around edges. Using a spoon, remove air pockets by pushing down evenly over entire hot crust. Immediately sprinkle marshmallows over top. Return to oven for 2–3 minutes more; remove and cool.

In a small saucepan, melt the peanut butter chips and 3 tablespoons butter. Stir in the corn syrup. Bring mixture to a light boil, stirring occasionally. Remove pan from heat and pour mixture over the marshmallow layer. Sprinkle peanuts evenly over top. Cool completely and cut into bars before serving.

Chocolaty
Cakes

Cookies-and-Cream Cake

Makes 15–18 servings

1 white cake mix
1¼ cups water
⅓ cup vegetable oil
3 egg whites
1½ cups Oreo cookies,
  crushed

Frosting
1 container vanilla
  frosting
1 ½ cups Oreo cookies,
  crushed

Preheat oven to 350 degrees.

In a bowl, mix together the cake mix, water, oil, and egg whites until smooth; gently stir in crushed cookies. Pour batter into greased-and-floured 9 x 13-inch pan. Bake for 25–35 minutes, or until a toothpick inserted into the center comes out clean; cool completely.

In a separate bowl, mix together the frosting and cookies; spread over cake.

Chocolate Toffee Cake

Makes 15–18 servings

1 chocolate cake mix
1 (14-ounce) can sweet-
    ened condensed milk
1 (12-ounce) jar caramel
    or butterscotch ice
    cream topping
1 (12-ounce) container
    whipped topping
4 Heath or Skor bars,
    chopped

In a bowl, prepare cake according to package directions and then bake in a 9 x 13-inch pan. While cake is still hot, use a wooden spoon handle to poke holes all over the cake. Pour condensed milk evenly over the cake. Pour the butterscotch topping evenly over that. Sprinkle half the candy bars over top. Refrigerate for at least 3 hours. Spread whipped topping over cake, then sprinkle with remaining candy bar pieces.

Butterfinger Cake

Makes 15–18 servings

1 German chocolate
cake mix
1 (8- to 12-ounce) jar
butterscotch ice
cream topping
4 Butterfinger bars,
crushed
1 (12-ounce) container
whipped topping
½ cup chopped pecans

In a bowl, prepare cake according to package directions and then bake in a 9 x 13-inch pan. While cake is still hot, use a wooden spoon handle to poke holes all over the cake. Pour butterscotch topping over cake and let it soak in; cool completely. Reserve one crushed Butterfinger bar and mix the rest into whipped topping along with the nuts. Spread over cooled cake. Sprinkle remaining Butterfinger pieces over top. Refrigerate until ready to serve.

Cherry Chunk Cake

Makes 15–18 servings

1 chocolate cake mix
2 eggs
1 (21-ounce) can
    cherry pie filling
¾ cup chopped nuts
¾ cup chocolate chips
½ cup brown sugar

Preheat oven to 350 degrees.

In a bowl, mix together the cake mix, eggs, and pie filling. Pour batter into a greased 9 x 13-inch pan. Sprinkle the nuts, chocolate chips, and brown sugar over top. Bake for 30–35 minutes.

Chocolate Pudding Poke Cake

Makes 15–18 servings

1 chocolate cake mix
2 small boxes instant
    chocolate pudding
4 cups cold milk

In a bowl, prepare cake according to package directions and then bake in a 9 x 13-inch pan. While cake is still hot, use a wooden spoon handle to poke holes at 1-inch intervals to the bottom of the cake.

In a separate bowl, use a wire whisk to beat together the pudding mixes and milk for 2 minutes. Quickly pour half of the thin pudding mixture over the warm cake and into the holes. Refrigerate remaining pudding mixture until slightly thick. Spoon over top of cake, swirling to frost. Refrigerate for at least 1 hour. Store in refrigerator.

NOTE: Other yummy flavor combinations include white or yellow cake mix with chocolate, butterscotch, pistachio, cheesecake, or vanilla pudding; chocolate cake mix with vanilla, cheesecake, or pistachio pudding; and lemon cake mix with lemon, vanilla, or cheesecake pudding.

Marshmallow Chocolate Chip Cake

Makes 15–18 servings

1 yellow cake mix
1 small box instant
   vanilla pudding
3 eggs
1 cup water
1/4 cup vegetable oil
1/4 cup applesauce
3/4 cup semisweet
   chocolate chips

Topping
1 cup mini
   marshmallows
1 container chocolate
   frosting
1/4 cup semisweet
   chocolate chips

Preheat oven to 350 degrees.

In a bowl, mix together the cake mix, pudding mix, eggs, water, oil, and applesauce until smooth. Stir in chocolate chips. Pour into a greased-and-floured 9 x 13-inch pan. Bake for 40–45 minutes, or until a toothpick inserted into the center comes out clean.

Immediately arrange marshmallows evenly over hot cake. Place frosting in a microwave-safe bowl and then microwave on high for 25–30 seconds. Stir until smooth and then drizzle over marshmallows. Sprinkle chocolate chips over top and cool completely.

Chocolate Lover's Cake

Makes 15–18 servings

Preheat oven to 350 degrees.

1 devil's food cake mix
1 small box instant
    chocolate pudding
1 (12-ounce) can
    lemon-lime soda
1/3 cup vegetable oil
4 eggs
1 container chocolate
    frosting

In a bowl, use an electric mixer to combine the cake mix, pudding mix, soda, oil, and eggs. Pour batter into a greased 9 x 13-inch pan. Bake for 30–35 minutes, or until a toothpick inserted into the center comes out clean. Cool and frost with chocolate frosting.

Just Like Snickers Cake

Makes 15–18 servings

1 German chocolate
    cake mix
1 (12-ounce) jar caramel
    ice cream topping
1 cup milk chocolate
    chips
3/4 cup chopped nuts

In a bowl, prepare cake according to package directions and then bake in a 9 x 13-inch pan. While still hot, poke holes all over top and then pour caramel topping over cake. Sprinkle the chocolate chips and nuts over top. Can serve cooled or while still warm.

Upside-Down German Chocolate Cake

Makes 15–18 *servings*

1 cup coconut
1 cup chopped nuts
1/2 cup milk chocolate
    chips
1 German chocolate
    cake mix
3/4 cup butter or
    margarine
1 (8-ounce) package
    cream cheese,
    softened
1 pound powdered sugar

Preheat oven to 350 degrees.

In a bowl, toss together the coconut and nuts and then evenly spread in the bottom of a greased 9 x 13-inch pan. Sprinkle chocolate chips over top.

In a separate bowl, prepare cake according to package directions; pour batter over coconut layer.

In another bowl, use an electric mixer to beat together the butter and cream cheese until smooth. Gradually add the powdered sugar, mixing well. Spoon mixture at even intervals over the cake batter. Bake for 40–50 minutes, or until a toothpick inserted into the center comes out clean. Invert cake onto a large platter and serve.

Chocolate Coconut Cake

Makes 15–18 servings

1 dark chocolate
   cake mix
1 cup milk
1 cup sugar
24 large marshmallows
1½ cups coconut

Topping
1½ cups sugar
½ cup evaporated milk
½ cup butter or
   margarine
1½ cups chocolate chips

In a bowl, prepare cake according to package directions. Pour batter onto a large sheet-cake pan and bake for the regular allotted time specified on box for cake pans, about 20–25 minutes.

In a saucepan, mix together the milk, sugar, and marshmallows and heat until the marshmallows are melted. Remove from heat and stir in the coconut. Spread mixture over warm cake.

In a separate saucepan, combine all topping ingredients except the chocolate chips and bring to a boil. Remove from heat and stir in chocolate chips until melted. Spread over top of cake.

Chocolate Marble Cake

Makes 15–18 servings

1 triple chocolate fudge
  cake mix
³/₄ cup butter or
  margarine
1 (8-ounce) package
  cream cheese,
  softened
1 pound powdered sugar

Preheat oven to 350 degrees.

In a bowl, prepare cake according to package directions and then bake in a greased-and-floured 9 x 13-inch pan.

In separate bowl, beat together the butter, cream cheese, and powdered sugar until smooth. Spoon over top of cake batter. Bake for 45–50 minutes; cool completely. Store in refrigerator.

Caramel-Pecan Chocolate Cake

Makes 15–18 *servings*

1 chocolate cake mix
1 (14-ounce) can sweet-
    ened condensed milk
1 (12-ounce) jar caramel
    ice cream topping
3/4 cup chopped pecans,
    divided
1 (12-ounce) container
    whipped topping

Preheat oven to 350 degrees.

In a bowl, prepare cake according to package directions and then bake in a greased 9 x 13-inch pan. Let cake cool about 30 minutes and then poke holes all over cake top with the handle of a wooden spoon. Pour condensed milk evenly over cake, followed by the caramel topping. Sprinkle 1/2 cup pecans over top. Chill 2–3 hours. Spread whipped topping over cake and sprinkle remaining pecans over top.

Cherry-Chocolate Cake

Makes 15–18 *servings*

1 chocolate cake mix
1 cup water
1 egg
1 (21-ounce) can
    cherry pie filling

Preheat oven to 350 degrees.

In a bowl, mix together the cake mix, water, and egg until smooth. Fold in the cherry pie filling. Pour into a greased 9 x 13-inch pan. Bake for 30–35 minutes, or until cake springs back when touched.

Peppermint Cake

Makes 15–18 *servings*

1 chocolate cake mix
1/2 cup crushed
    peppermint candy
1 container chocolate
    frosting
2 1/2 tablespoons crushed
    peppermint candy

Preheat oven to 350 degrees.

In a bowl, prepare cake according to package directions. Stir in 1/2 cup crushed candy. Pour batter into a greased 9 x 13-inch pan. Bake as directed; cool completely. Spread frosting over cooled cake; sprinkle with 2 1/2 tablespoons crushed candy.

Peanut M&M Cake

Makes 15–18 *servings*

1 chocolate or yellow
    cake mix
½ cup flour
1 cup peanut M&Ms
1 container white
    frosting
¼ cup creamy peanut
    butter
Peanut M&Ms, to
    garnish

Preheat oven to 350 degrees.

In a bowl, prepare cake according to package directions. Stir in flour and M&Ms. Pour batter into a greased 9 x 13-inch pan. Bake for 30–35 minutes, or until a toothpick inserted into the center comes out clean; cool completely.

In a separate bowl, mix together the frosting and peanut butter. Frost cooled cake and then decorate with more M&Ms.

Peanut Butter–Chocolate Chip Cake

Makes 15–18 *servings*

1 white cake mix
1/2 cup chunky peanut butter
1 cup chocolate chips
1 container chocolate frosting
1/4 cup creamy peanut butter
1/2 cup chopped nuts (optional)

Preheat oven to 350 degrees.

In a bowl, prepare cake according to package directions. Beat in the chunky peanut butter with an electric mixer. Stir in the chocolate chips. Pour batter into a greased 9 x 13-inch pan. Bake for 25–30 minutes, or until a toothpick inserted into the center comes out clean; cool completely.

In a separate bowl, mix together the frosting and creamy peanut butter. Spread over top of cooled cake and then garnish with nuts, if desired.

Chocolate Chip Carrot Cake

Makes 15–18 servings

1 spice cake mix
3 eggs
⅓ cup vegetable oil
1¼ cups water
1 cup shredded carrot
½ cup chopped walnuts
½ cup coconut
1 cup chocolate chips
1 container cream
   cheese frosting

Preheat oven to 350 degrees.

In a bowl, use an electric mixer at low speed to beat together the cake mix, eggs, oil, water, and carrot for 2 minutes. Stir in the nuts, coconut, and chocolate chips. Pour batter into a greased-and-floured 9 x 13-inch pan. Bake for 27–35 minutes, or until a toothpick inserted into the center comes out clean; cool for 15–20 minutes and then spread frosting over top.

Chocolate Zucchini Nut Cake

Makes 15–18 servings

1 chocolate or yellow
   cake mix
3 eggs
¼ cup vegetable oil
¼ cup applesauce
½ cup water
2 cups peeled and
   grated zucchini*
¾ cup mini chocolate
   chips
½ cup chopped walnuts
1 container chocolate
   or cream cheese
   frosting

Preheat oven to 350 degrees.

In a bowl, beat together the cake mix, eggs, oil, applesauce, and water. Stir in the zucchini, chocolate chips, and nuts. Pour batter into a greased-and-floured 9 x 13-inch pan. Bake for 28–33 minutes, or until a toothpick inserted into the center comes out clean. Spread frosting over cooled cake or sprinkle with powdered sugar.

*If using large zucchini, remove seeds before grating. Approximate 2½ to 3 small zucchini yields 2 cups grated.

Fruity Cakes

Apple Spice Cake

Makes 15–18 servings

3 cups sliced apples
1/2 cup raisins
1/2 cup water
1 small box vanilla or French vanilla cook-and-serve pudding*
1 spice cake mix
1/2 cup chopped nuts (optional)
Powdered sugar

Preheat oven to 350 degrees.

Cut apple slices into bite-size pieces. Mix together the apples, raisins, water, and pudding mix in a microwave-safe bowl. Microwave on high for 4 minutes. Stir and spread apple mixture evenly over bottom of a greased 9 x 13-inch pan.

Prepare cake according to package directions. Pour over the apples. Sprinkle nuts over top, if desired. Bake for 30–40 minutes, or until a toothpick inserted into the center comes out clean; cool 20 minutes. Sprinkle powdered sugar over top.

NOTE: Try butterscotch pudding with a white cake mix in place of vanilla pudding and spice cake mix.

*Do not use instant pudding in this recipe.

Berry Delight Cake

Makes 15–18 *servings*

**1 white or vanilla
   cake mix**
3 eggs
1/2 cup sour cream
3/4 cup water
1/2 cup applesauce
**1 (15-ounce) can
   blueberries or
   blackberries, drained
   and rinsed**

Topping
**1 (8-ounce) container
   whipped topping**
**1 (6-ounce) container
   blueberry or
   blackberry yogurt**

Preheat oven to 350 degrees.

In a bowl, use an electric mixer to mix together the cake mix, eggs, sour cream, water, and applesauce for 2 minutes until smooth. Using a rubber spatula, gently fold in the berries. Pour batter into a greased-and-floured 9 x 13-inch pan. Bake for 30–35 minutes, or until a toothpick inserted into the center comes out clean; let cool completely. Cover and chill for 2–3 hours.

Before serving, gently stir the whipped topping and yogurt together; frost cake. Store in refrigerator.

Peaches-and-Cream Cake

Makes 15–18 servings

1 white cake mix
1 small box peach
   gelatin
2 eggs
1¼ cups peach juice
   (drained from
   peaches)*
⅓ cup vegetable oil
1 (29-ounce) can
   sliced peaches,
   juice drained and
   reserved, divided
1 (12-ounce) container
   whipped topping

Preheat oven to 350 degrees.

In a bowl, use an electric mixer to beat together the cake mix, gelatin, eggs, juice, and oil for 1–2 minutes. Cut enough peach slices into chunks to measure 1¼ cups; reserve remaining peaches. Mix the peach chunks into the batter. Pour into a greased 9 x 13-inch pan. Bake for 30–35 minutes, or until a toothpick inserted into the center comes out clean; let cool. Cover and refrigerate for 2–3 hours.

Before serving, spread the whipped topping over cake. Arrange the reserved peach slices over top. Store in refrigerator.

*If there is not enough peach juice in can, add water to make up the difference.

Pineapple Coconut Cream Cake

Makes 15–18 servings

1 white or yellow
   cake mix
4 eggs
1 (20-ounce) can
   crushed pineapple,
   with juice
1/2 cup vegetable oil
2 cups coconut, divided
1 (12-ounce) container
   whipped topping
1 (8-ounce) can crushed
   pineapple, with juice
1 small box instant
   coconut cream
   pudding

Preheat oven to 350 degrees.

In a bowl, mix together the cake mix, eggs, large can of pineapple, and oil. Stir in 1 cup coconut. Pour batter into a greased 9 x 13-inch pan. Bake for 30–35 minutes, or until a toothpick inserted into the center comes out clean. Chill for at least 2 hours.

Before serving, mix together the whipped topping, small can of pineapple, and pudding mix until smooth. Spread over cake. Sprinkle remaining coconut over top. Store in refrigerator.

Pineapple Upside Down Cake

Makes 15–18 *servings*

Preheat oven to 350 degrees.

½ cup butter or
  margarine
¾ cup firmly packed
  brown sugar
1 (20-ounce) can
  pineapple slices,
  juice reserved
1 small jar maraschino
  cherries, drained and
  halved
1 yellow or white
  cake mix

Melt the butter in a 9 x 13-inch pan. Sprinkle brown sugar evenly over butter. Arrange the pineapple slices over the brown sugar. Place the cherry halves in the middle of each pineapple ring; set aside.

Prepare the cake according to package directions, using the reserved pineapple juice instead of the water called for on box. Pour batter over the pineapple. Bake for 35–45 minutes, or until a toothpick inserted into the center comes out clean. Let stand in pan for 5 minutes and then invert hot cake onto a serving platter.

Blueberry Swirl Cake

Makes 15–18 servings

1 white cake mix
1/3 cup oil
2 eggs
3/4 cup water
1 (21-ounce) can
    blueberry pie filling
1 (8-ounce) package
    cream cheese,
    softened
1 cup powdered sugar
1 (12-ounce) container
    whipped topping

Preheat oven to 350 degrees.

In a bowl, mix together the cake mix, oil, eggs, and water. Stir in the pie filling. Pour batter into a greased 9 x 13-inch pan. Bake for 30–35 minutes, or until a toothpick inserted into the center comes out clean; let cool.

Before serving, mix together the cream cheese, powdered sugar, and whipped topping. Spread over cake. Store in refrigerator.

Raspberry Cream Cheese Cake

Makes 15–18 servings

1 white cake mix
1 small box raspberry
    gelatin
1 cup boiling water
½ cup cold water
1 (8-ounce) package
    cream cheese,
    softened
1 (8-ounce) container
    whipped topping
1 (21-ounce) can
    raspberry pie filling

Prepare cake according to package directions. Pour batter into a greased 9 x 13-inch pan. Bake as directed and let cool. Use a fork to poke deep holes into cake about 1 inch apart.

Dissolve the gelatin in 1 cup boiling water; add the cold water. Slowly pour gelatin mixture over the cake and into the holes.

In a bowl, mix together the cream cheese and whipped topping. Spread over the cake. Spoon the pie filling evenly over top. Refrigerate for at least 3 hours before serving. Store in refrigerator.

Moist Carrot Nut Cake

Makes 15–18 servings

1 carrot cake mix
6 egg whites
1 (20-ounce) can
    crushed pineapple,
    with juice
½ cup olive oil
½ cup grated or
    chopped nuts
1 container cream
    cheese frosting or
    powdered sugar

Preheat oven to 350 degrees.

In a bowl, use an electric mixer to beat together the cake mix, egg whites, pineapple, and oil. Stir in the nuts. Pour batter into a greased 9 x 13-inch pan. Bake for 28–35 minutes, or until a toothpick inserted into the center comes out clean; let cool for 15–20 minutes. Frost cake with cream cheese frosting or sprinkle powdered sugar over top.

White Chocolate Strawberry Cake

Makes 12 servings

1 strawberry cake mix
1 cup white chocolate chips
1 large box instant white chocolate or vanilla pudding
1 (8-ounce) container whipped topping
Sliced strawberries

Preheat oven to 350 degrees.

Prepare cake according to package directions. Stir in the white chocolate chips. Pour batter into a greased 9 x 13-inch pan. Bake as directed; let cool.

Make pudding according to package directions; chill until set. Cut cake into 24 thin slices, about 1½ x 3 inches each. Place a slice of cake on a small plate. Top with a large scoop of pudding. Place another slice of cake over top. Add more pudding. Top with a dollop of whipped topping and strawberries.

Sweet Cherry Pie Cake

Makes 15–18 *servings*

1 white cake mix
⅓ cup oil
2 eggs
½ cup water
**1 (21-ounce) can
    cherry pie filling**
1½ tablespoons milk
1 cup powdered sugar

Preheat oven to 350 degrees.

In a bowl, mix together the cake mix, oil, eggs, and water. Pour batter into greased 9 x 13-inch pan. Swirl in the pie filling. Bake for 30–35 minutes; let cool.

In a bowl, mix together the milk and powdered sugar; drizzle over cake.

Applesauce Cake

Makes 15–18 *servings*

1 spice cake mix
2 cups applesauce
¼ cup oil
2 eggs
**¼ cup wheat germ
    (optional)**
**1 container vanilla
    or cream cheese
    frosting**

Preheat oven to 350 degrees.

In a bowl, mix together the cake mix, applesauce, oil, and eggs. Stir in the wheat germ, if desired. Pour into a greased 9 x 13-inch pan. Bake for 35–40 minutes; let cool. Top with frosting.

Lemon-Lime Cake

Makes **15–18** *servings*

1 lemon cake mix
1 small package lime
    gelatin
1 cup boiling water
1/2 cup cold water
1 small box instant
    lemon pudding
1 (8-ounce) container
    whipped topping

Preheat oven to 350 degrees.

Prepare cake according to package directions. Pour batter into a greased 9 x 13-inch pan. Bake as directed; let cool. Use a fork to poke deep holes into cake about 1 inch apart. Dissolve gelatin in the boiling water; stir in the cold water. Slowly pour gelatin mixture over cake and into holes.

In a bowl, mix together the pudding mix and whipped topping until stiff. Immediately frost cake. Refrigerate for at least 2–3 hours and served chilled. Store in refrigerator.

Easy Apple Pie Cake

Makes 15–18 *servings*

1 white cake mix
1/3 cup oil
2 eggs
1/2 cup water
1 (21-ounce) can
　apple pie filling

Glaze
1 tablespoon butter or
　margarine, melted
1 cup powdered sugar
1/2 teaspoon vanilla
Hot water

Preheat oven to 350 degrees.

In a bowl, mix together the cake mix, oil, eggs, and water. Pour mixture into a greased 9 x 13-inch pan. Swirl in the apple pie filling. Bake for 30–35 minutes.

In a bowl, mix together the butter, powdered sugar, and vanilla. Stir in hot water by the teaspoon until desired consistency is reached. Drizzle glaze over cake.

Banana Split Cake

Makes 15–18 *servings*

Preheat oven to 350 degrees.

1/4 teaspoon baking soda
3/4 cup buttermilk
1 white cake mix
1/4 cup water
2 bananas, mashed
2 tablespoons
    vegetable oil
3 egg whites, whipped
1/2 cup chopped walnuts,
    divided
3/4 cup hot fudge topping

In a bowl, dissolve the baking soda in the buttermilk. Add the cake mix, water, bananas, oil, and egg whites. Spoon half the batter into a greased-and-floured 9 x 13-inch pan. Sprinkle 1/4 cup walnuts evenly over batter. Drizzle hot fudge over the walnuts. Top with remaining batter. Sprinkle remaining walnuts over top. Bake for 30 minutes, or until lightly browned; let cool.

Piña Colada Cake

Makes **15–18** *servings*

1 yellow cake mix
1 (20-ounce) can
crushed pineapple,
    drained
1 (14-ounce) can sweet-
    ened condensed milk
1 (8-ounce) container
    whipped topping
²/₃ cup coconut

Prepare cake according to package directions. Mix half of the pineapple into the batter. Pour into a greased 9 x 13-inch pan. Bake as directed. Use a fork to poke holes all over warm cake about 1 inch apart. Pour the sweetened condensed milk evenly over cake and into the holes; let cool. Spread the whipped topping over cake. Sprinkle with the coconut and remaining pineapple.

Fruit Cocktail Cake

Makes 15–18 servings

Preheat oven to 350 degrees.

1 yellow cake mix
1 small box instant
vanilla pudding
1 (15-ounce) can fruit
cocktail, with syrup
3/4 cup coconut
3 large eggs
1/4 cup oil
1/2 cup light brown sugar
1/2 cup chopped nuts
1/2 cup butter
1/2 cup sugar
1/2 cup evaporated milk
1 cup coconut
1 (8-ounce) container
whipped topping

In a bowl, use an electric mixer to beat together the cake mix, pudding mix, fruit cocktail, 3/4 coconut, eggs, and oil for 3–5 minutes. Pour into a greased 9 x 13-inch pan. Sprinkle brown sugar and nuts over top. Bake for 30–35 minutes; let cool 15 minutes.

In a small saucepan, combine the butter, sugar, and evaporated milk; boil for 2 minutes. Stir in 1 cup coconut and then pour over cake. Serve warm or cool with a dollop of whipped topping.

Orange-Pineapple Layer Cake

Makes 12–15 servings

1 yellow cake mix
$1/3$ cup vegetable oil
3 tablespoons water
3 large eggs
1 small can mandarin
   oranges, with juice

Filling
1 (12-ounce) container
   whipped topping
1 large box instant
   vanilla pudding
1 (8-ounce) can crushed
   pineapple, with juice

Preheat oven to 350 degrees.

In a bowl, mix together the cake mix, oil, water, eggs, and oranges. Pour batter into three greased-and-floured 8-inch round pans. Bake for 23–25 minutes, or until cake springs back when touched.

In a bowl, use a spoon to mix together the whipped topping, pudding mix, and pineapple. Spread the filling between each layer of cake and on top and sides. Store in refrigerator.

Sweet Tropical Cake

Makes 15–18 servings

Preheat oven to 350 degrees.

1 yellow cake mix
3 eggs
1/2 cup vegetable oil
1/2 cup applesauce
1 small can mandarin
    oranges, drained
1 cup crushed
    pineapple, with juice
3 tablespoons
    cornstarch
1 cup sugar

Topping

1 small box instant
    vanilla pudding
2 cups milk
1 (8-ounce) container
    whipped topping
4 bananas, sliced
1/3 cup coconut

In a bowl, mix together the cake mix, eggs, oil, applesauce, and oranges until smooth. Pour into a greased 9 x 13-inch pan. Bake for 30–35 minutes, or until a toothpick inserted into the center comes out clean; let cool.

In a small saucepan, mix together the pineapple, cornstarch, and sugar. Cook over medium heat, stirring constantly, until thick and clear. Pour over cake.

In a bowl, use a wire whisk to beat together the pudding mix and milk for 2 minutes. Chill for 5 minutes to set. Fold in the whipped topping.

Just before serving, place the bananas on top of the pineapple layer. Spread pudding mixture over top and then sprinkle with coconut.

Peach Cream Cheese Cake

Makes 15–18 servings

1 white cake mix
1 (21-ounce) can
    peach pie filling
3 eggs
½ cup sour cream
1 (8-ounce) package
    cream cheese,
    softened
1 small box instant
    vanilla pudding
1 (20-ounce) can
    crushed pineapple,
    with juice
1 (8-ounce) container
    whipped topping

In a bowl, use a fork to mix together the cake mix, pie filling, and eggs. Gently stir in the sour cream. Pour batter into a greased 9 x 13-inch glass pan. Bake for 30–35 minutes; cool completely.

In a separate bowl, mix together the cream cheese, pudding mix, and pineapple. Gently fold in the whipped topping. Spread over cake and chill until ready to serve. Store in refrigerator.

Apple-Spice Sour Cream Cake

Makes 15–18 servings

1 spice cake mix
3 small apples, peeled, cored, and chopped
1 (14-ounce) can sweetened condensed milk
1 cup sour cream
¼ cup lemon juice
1 teaspoon ground cinnamon

Preheat oven to 350 degrees.

Prepare cake according to package directions. Stir in the apples. Pour into a greased 9 x 13-inch pan. Bake for 28–30 minutes. Top with a mixture of the condensed milk, sour cream, and lemon juice. Return to oven and bake for 8–10 minutes more, or until done. Sprinkle the cinnamon over top; let cool. Store in refrigerator.

Hawaiian Pudding Cake

Makes 15–18 *servings*

1 yellow cake mix
1 large box instant
  vanilla pudding
1 (8-ounce) package
  cream cheese,
  softened
1 (20-ounce) can
  pineapple chunks,
  drained
1 (12-ounce) container
  whipped topping
⅓ cup coconut

Prepare cake according to package directions. Pour into a greased 9 x 13-inch pan. Bake as directed; let cool.

In a bowl, make pudding according to package directions. Stir in cream cheese. Pour pudding mixture onto cake. Sprinkle pineapple over pudding. Cover with whipped topping and then sprinkle with coconut. Store in refrigerator.

Apple Streusel Cake

Makes 15–18 *servings*

Preheat oven to 350 degrees.

1 yellow cake mix
2 large eggs
1/2 teaspoon lemon
    extract
1 (21-ounce) can
    apple pie filling
1/4 cup butter or
    margarine, melted
1/2 cup sugar
1/2 cup flour
1/2 teaspoon cinnamon

In a bowl, mix together the cake mix, eggs, lemon extract, and pie filling. Pour batter into a greased 9 x 13-inch pan.

In a bowl, combine the butter, sugar, flour, and cinnamon. Mix with a fork until crumbly. Sprinkle mixture over cake batter and then bake for 42–47 minutes.

Strawberry-Banana Poke Cake

Makes 15–18 servings

1 white cake mix
1 small box strawberry-banana gelatin
1 cup boiling water
½ cup cold water
1 (8-ounce) container whipped topping
Sliced strawberries and bananas (optional)

Prepare cake according to package directions; let cool. Use a fork to poke holes all over the top of cake.

In a bowl, stir the gelatin with the boiling water until dissolved. Stir in the cold water and then pour over the cake and into the holes. Chill for 4 hours. Spread whipped topping over cake before serving. Store in the refrigerator. Serve with sliced strawberries and bananas, if desired.

Strawberry Cream Cake

Makes 15–18 *servings*

1 French vanilla or
  strawberry cake mix
2 (10-ounce) bags frozen
  sliced strawberries,
  thawed and
  sweetened
1 small box instant
  French vanilla or
  cheesecake pudding
1 (8-ounce) container
  whipped topping

Preheat oven to 350 degrees.

Prepare cake according to package directions. Pour batter into a greased 9 x 13-inch pan. Bake as directed; let cool. Using the handle of a wooden spoon, poke holes all over cake about 1 inch apart. Pour the strawberries and juice over the cake and spread the strawberries to cover.

In a bowl, prepare pudding according to package directions. Smooth pudding over the berries. Spread the whipped topping over top. Store in refrigerator.

Raspberry Yogurt Cake

Makes 15–18 servings

1 white cake mix
1 (6-ounce) container
    raspberry yogurt*

Topping
1 (8-ounce) container
    whipped topping
1 (6-ounce) container
    raspberry yogurt

Preheat oven to 350 degrees.

Prepare the cake according to package directions. Gently stir in yogurt. Pour batter into a greased 9 x 13-inch pan. Bake for 30–35 minutes, or until a toothpick inserted into the center comes out clean; let cool for 15–20 minutes and then chill for 4 hours.

In a bowl, mix together the whipped topping and yogurt. Spread over the cake. Store in refrigerator.

*Blueberry, boysenberry, and lemon yogurt also work.

Lemonade Cake

Makes 15–18 servings

1 lemon cake mix
1 cup frozen lemonade
    concentrate, thawed
1 cup powdered sugar
1 container lemon or
    vanilla frosting

Preheat oven to 350 degrees.

Prepare cake according to package directions. Pour batter into a greased 9 x 13-inch pan; cool for 15 minutes. Use a fork to poke holes all over top of warm cake.

In a bowl, stir together the lemonade concentrate and powdered sugar. Drizzle lemonade mixture evenly over top; refrigerate until cold. Spread frosting over cold cake. Cover and refrigerate until ready to serve.

Original Gelatin Poke Cake

Makes 15–18 servings

1 white cake mix
1 small box gelatin, any flavor
1 cup boiling water
½ cup cold water
1 (8-ounce) container whipped topping

Prepare cake according to package directions. Pour batter into a greased 9 x 13-inch pan. Bake as directed; let cool. Use a fork to poke holes all over top of cake.

In a bowl, dissolve the gelatin in the boiling water. Stir in the cold water. Pour gelatin over cake and into the holes. Chill for 4 hours. Spread whipped topping over cake. Store in refrigerator.

Bundt
Cakes

Vanilla Spice Cake

Makes 16 *servings*

¾ cup sour cream
4 eggs
½ cup water
½ cup oil
1 spice cake mix
1 small box instant
   vanilla pudding
Powdered sugar

Preheat oven to 350 degrees.

In a bowl, beat together the sour cream, eggs, water, and oil. Add the cake and pudding mixes. Pour batter into a greased tube or Bundt cake pan. Bake for 45–50 minutes, or until a toothpick inserted into the center comes out clean. Invert hot cake onto a platter; let cool. When cool, sift powdered sugar over cake.

Cherry Swirl Cake

Makes 16 *servings*

1 white cake mix
3 eggs
2 (21-ounce) cans
   cherry pie filling
1 (8-ounce) container
   whipped topping

Preheat oven to 350 degrees.

In a bowl, mix together the cake mix and eggs. Stir in 1 can of pie filling. Pour batter into a greased tube or Bundt cake pan. Bake for 40–50 minutes, or until a toothpick inserted into the center comes out clean. Invert hot cake onto a platter; let cool. Serve individual pieces with a scoop of the remaining pie filling and a dollop of whipped topping.

Banana Pudding Cake

Makes 16 *servings*

1 small box instant
  banana pudding
1½ cups milk
1 spice cake mix
⅓ cup vegetable oil
3 eggs
2 bananas, mashed
1 container cream
  cheese frosting or
  powdered sugar

Preheat oven to 350 degrees.

In a bowl, mix together the pudding mix and milk until thick. Stir in the cake mix, oil, and eggs. Add the bananas. Pour batter into a greased tube or Bundt cake pan. Bake for 45–50 minutes, or until a toothpick inserted into the comes out clean. Invert hot cake onto a platter; let cool. When cool, spread the frosting or sift powdered sugar over cake.

Easy Blueberry Bundt

Makes 16 *servings*

1 white cake mix
3 eggs
1 (21-ounce) can
  blueberry pie filling
1 (8-ounce) container
  whipped topping

Preheat oven to 350 degrees.

In a bowl, mix together the cake mix and eggs. Stir in the pie filling. Pour batter into a greased tube or Bundt cake pan. Bake for 40–50 minutes, or until a toothpick inserted into the center comes out clean. Invert hot cake onto a platter; let cool. Serve individual pieces with a dollop of whipped topping.

White Chocolate Raspberry Cake

Makes **16** *servings*

1 white cake mix
3 eggs
1 (21-ounce) can
   raspberry pie filling
1 cup white chocolate
   chips
1 (8-ounce) container
   whipped topping
1 white chocolate bar,
   grated
½ cup chopped or
   grated nuts

Preheat oven to 350 degrees.

In a bowl, mix together the cake mix and eggs. Stir in the pie filling and white chocolate chips. Pour batter into a greased tube or Bundt cake pan. Bake for 40–50 minutes, or until a toothpick inserted into the center comes out clean. Invert hot cake onto a platter; let cool. Serve individual pieces with a dollop of whipped topping and a sprinkle of chocolate and nuts over top.

Strawberry Sour Cream Cake

Makes 16 servings

3/4 cup sour cream
4 eggs
1/2 cup water
1/2 cup oil
1 strawberry cake mix
1 small box instant
    cheesecake or vanilla
    pudding
1 cup white chocolate or
    vanilla chips
Powdered sugar
1 (8-ounce) container
    whipped topping
Strawberries, sliced

Preheat oven to 350 degrees.

In a bowl, beat together the sour cream, eggs, water, and oil. Add the cake and pudding mixes. Stir in white chocolate chips. Pour batter into a greased tube or Bundt cake pan. Bake for 45–50 minutes, or until a toothpick inserted into the center comes out clean. Invert hot cake onto a platter; let cool. When cool, sift powdered sugar over top. Serve individual pieces with a dollop of whipped topping and strawberries over top.

Pumpkin Caramel Cake

Makes **16** *servings*

Preheat oven to 350 degrees.

1 spice or butter pecan
   cake mix
¼ cup applesauce
2 eggs
1 (15-ounce) can
   pumpkin
1 (12-ounce) jar caramel
   ice cream topping
1 (8-ounce) container
   whipped topping

In a bowl, mix together the cake mix, applesauce, and eggs. Stir in the pumpkin. Pour batter into a greased tube or Bundt cake pan. Bake for 38–45 minutes, or until a toothpick inserted into the center comes out clean. Invert hot cake onto a platter; let cool. Drizzle individual pieces of cake with caramel and a dollop of whipped topping over top.

Spiced Caramel Apple Bundt

Makes 16 servings

1 spice cake mix
3 eggs
1 (21-ounce) can
apple pie filling
1 (8-ounce) jar caramel
ice cream topping

Preheat oven to 350 degrees.

In a bowl, mix together the cake mix and eggs. Stir in the pie filling. Pour batter into a greased tube or Bundt cake pan. Bake for 40–50 minutes or until a toothpick inserted into the center comes out clean. Invert hot cake onto a platter; let cool. When cool, drizzle caramel topping over top.

Lemon Pie Cake

Makes **16** *servings*

1 white or lemon
   cake mix
3 eggs
1 (15-ounce) can
   lemon pie filling
1 container white
   frosting or powdered
   sugar

Preheat oven to 350 degrees.

In a bowl, mix together the cake mix and eggs. Stir in the pie filling. Pour batter into a greased tube or Bundt cake pan. Bake for 45–50 minutes, or until a toothpick inserted into the center comes out clean. Invert hot cake onto a platter; let cool. When cool, spread frosting or sift powdered sugar over top.

Lemon Poppy Seed Cake

Makes **16** servings

1 lemon cake mix
1 small box instant
    lemon pudding
2 tablespoons poppy
    seeds
4 eggs
1/4 cup vegetable oil
1/4 cup applesauce
1 cup water

Glaze
1/3 cup lemon juice
1 1/3 cups powdered sugar

Preheat oven to 350 degrees.

In a bowl, mix together the cake mix, pudding mix, poppy seeds, eggs, oil, applesauce, and water until smooth. Pour batter into a greased tube or Bundt cake pan. Bake for 45–50 minutes. Invert hot cake onto a platter.

In a separate bowl, mix together the lemon juice and powdered sugar. Poke holes with a fork in the top of the hot cake and pour the glaze over top. Let glaze soak into cake for at least 5 minutes before serving.

Banana Sour Cream Cake

Makes **16** *servings*

2 bananas, mashed
1 white cake mix
1 small box instant vanilla pudding
3 eggs
1 cup sour cream
1/3 cup water
2 tablespoons oil
1/4 teaspoon baking powder
1 container cream cheese frosting

Preheat oven to 350 degrees.

In a bowl, combine the bananas, cake mix, pudding mix, eggs, sour cream, water, oil, and baking powder. Mix until just moistened. Pour batter into greased tube or Bundt cake pan. Bake for 45–50 minutes. Invert hot cake onto a platter; let cool. Place frosting in the microwave for 10–15 seconds to soften. Drizzle over cake and serve.

Perfect Pistachio Cake

Makes 16 servings

1 yellow cake mix
3 large eggs
1 cup club soda
2 small boxes instant
   pistachio pudding,
   divided
⅓ cup vegetable oil
1¼ cups finely chopped
   white pistachio nuts
   or pecans, divided
1 (12-ounce) container
   whipped topping

Preheat oven to 350 degrees.

In a bowl, combine the cake mix, eggs, club soda, 1 box pudding mix, oil, and ½ cup nuts. Mix well and pour into a greased tube or Bundt cake pan. Bake for 40–50 minutes, or until a toothpick inserted into the center comes out clean. Invert hot cake onto a platter; let cool.

In a bowl, fold together the remaining box of pudding mix and whipped topping. Spread evenly over cake. Sprinkle with remaining nuts.

Chocolate Pistachio Pound Cake

Makes **16** *servings*

1 white cake mix
1 small box instant
   pistachio pudding
$\frac{1}{2}$ cup orange juice
$\frac{1}{2}$ cup oil
$\frac{1}{2}$ cup water
3 large eggs
4 drops green food
   coloring
$\frac{1}{2}$ cup chocolate syrup,
   plus more

Preheat oven to 350 degrees.

In a bowl, mix together the cake mix, pudding mix, orange juice, oil, and water. Add eggs 1 at a time, mixing well after each addition. Stir in the food coloring. Pour all but 1$\frac{1}{2}$ cups of batter into a greased tube or Bundt cake pan. Mix chocolate syrup into the reserved batter. Pour over the batter in pan. Bake for 45–50 minutes, or until a toothpick inserted into the center comes out clean. Invert hot cake onto a platter; let cool. Serve individual pieces with chocolate syrup drizzled over top.

Death-by-Chocolate Cake

¾ cup sour cream
4 eggs
½ cup water
½ cup oil
1 chocolate cake mix
1 small box instant
   chocolate pudding
1 cup semisweet
   chocolate chips
Powdered sugar

Preheat oven to 350 degrees.

In a bowl, beat together the sour cream, eggs, water, and oil until smooth. Add the cake and pudding mixes. Stir in the chocolate chips. Pour batter into a greased tube or Bundt cake pan. Bake for 45–55 minutes, or until a toothpick inserted into the center comes out clean. Invert hot cake onto a platter; let cool. When cool, sift powdered sugar over top.

Chocolate Chip Cake

Makes **16** *servings*

1 yellow cake mix
1 small box instant
   vanilla pudding
1 cup sour cream
3 large eggs
1/4 cup vegetable oil
1/4 cup applesauce
1 cup semisweet
   chocolate chips,
   divided
1 cup chopped pecans,
   divided

Preheat oven to 350 degrees.

In a bowl, use an electric mixer to blend together the cake mix, pudding mix, sour cream, eggs, oil, and applesauce for 5–6 minutes. Grease a tube or Bundt cake pan. Pour one-third of the batter into pan and sprinkle half the chocolate chips and pecans over top. Pour in remaining batter and top with remaining chips and nuts. Bake for 50–55 minutes, or until a toothpick inserted into the center comes out clean. Cool for 5 minutes and then invert onto a platter; let cool.

Lemony Cream Cheese Cake

Makes **16** servings

1 (8-ounce) package cream cheese, softened
3 large eggs
1 yellow or lemon cake mix
1 small box instant lemon or vanilla pudding
3/4 cup milk
1/2 teaspoon lemon extract
2 tablespoons lemon zest

Preheat oven to 350 degrees.

In a bowl, use an electric mixer to beat the cream cheese until smooth and fluffy. Add eggs 1 at a time, beating well after each addition.

In a separate bowl, mix together the cake mix and pudding mix. In two or three intervals, add the cake mix powder alternately with the milk into the cream cheese. Beat just until smooth. Gently stir in the lemon extract and zest. Pour batter into a greased tube or Bundt cake pan. Bake for 45–50 minutes, or until a toothpick inserted into the center comes out clean. Invert hot cake onto a platter; let cool.

Luscious Lemon Cake

Makes **16** *servings*

1 yellow cake mix
1 small box instant
    lemon pudding
1 teaspoon lemon
    extract
3/4 cup water
1/2 cup vegetable oil
1/4 cup applesauce
4 eggs

Icing
1 cup powdered sugar
1/3 cup orange juice

Preheat oven to 350 degrees.

In a bowl, use an electric mixer to beat together the cake mix, pudding mix, lemon extract, water, oil, and applesauce until smooth. Add eggs one at a time, beating well after each addition. Beat on high speed for 8 minutes. Pour batter into a greased tube or Bundt cake pan. Bake for 45–50 minutes, or until a toothpick inserted into the center comes out clean. Invert hot cake onto a platter.

In a bowl, combine the powdered sugar and orange juice. Drizzle glaze over hot cake.

Orange-Pumpkin Cake

Makes 16 servings

1 yellow cake mix
3 egg whites
1¼ cups canned
    pumpkin
1 cup orange juice
⅓ cup sour cream
1½ teaspoons vanilla
1 teaspoon cinnamon
½ teaspoon nutmeg
½ teaspoon allspice

Glaze
1½ cups powdered sugar
¼ teaspoon vanilla
Water, as needed

Preheat oven to 350 degrees.

In a bowl, mix together all of the cake ingredients for 2–3 minutes. Pour into a greased tube or Bundt cake pan. Bake for 35–40 minutes. Invert hot cake onto a platter.

In a bowl, mix together the powdered sugar and vanilla, then gradually add water a tablespoon at a time until desired consistency is reached; drizzle over hot cake and let cool.

Crisps,
Cobblers,
Trifles,
& More

Quick and Easy Apple Crisp

Makes 15–18 *servings*

Preheat oven to 350 degrees.

4–6 apples (about 6 cups)
1 yellow cake mix
½ cup quick oats
2 tablespoons sugar
1 tablespoon cinnamon
½ cup butter or
    margarine, melted

Peel, core, and slice the apples. Spread over the bottom of a greased 8 x 8-inch pan.

In a bowl, mix together the cake mix, oats, sugar, and cinnamon. Pour butter over the top and mix with a fork until crumbly. Sprinkle over the apples. Bake for 35–40 minutes, or until apples are tender and top is golden brown.

Sweet Blueberry Cobbler

Makes 15–18 *servings*

1 yellow cake mix
1 (20-ounce) can
   crushed pineapple,
   with juice
1 (21-ounce) can
   blueberry pie filling
1/2 cup butter or
   margarine

Preheat oven to 350 degrees.

Grease a 9 x 13-inch pan. Sprinkle half of the cake mix evenly into bottom of pan. Pour pineapple over cake mix. Spoon pie filling over pineapple. Cover with remaining cake mix. With a sharp knife, cut the butter into small pieces and place evenly over top. Bake for 45–50 minutes, or until light golden brown.

Simple Peach Cobbler

Makes 15–18 servings

Preheat oven to 350 degrees.

1 yellow cake mix
1 (29-ounce) can sliced
   peaches, with juice
¼ to ½ cup butter or
   margarine, thinly
   sliced

Grease a 9 x 13-inch pan. Sprinkle half of the cake mix evenly into bottom of pan. Pour the peaches and juice evenly over cake mix. Cover with the remaining cake mix. Put butter slices over top. Bake for 50 minutes, or until light golden brown.

Cherry-Peach Cobbler

Makes 15–18 servings

Preheat oven to 350 degrees.

1 yellow cake mix
1 (21-ounce) can
   cherry pie filling
1 (29-ounce) can peach
   slices, juice drained
   and reserved

Grease a 9 x 13-inch pan. Sprinkle half of the cake mix evenly into bottom of pan. Spoon pie filling evenly over cake mix. Arrange the peach slices over pie filling. Cover with remaining cake mix. Pour peach juice over top. Bake for 47–52 minutes, or until light golden brown.

Easiest Apple Cobbler

Makes 15–18 servings

Preheat oven to 350 degrees.

1 yellow cake mix
1 (21-ounce) can
    apple pie filling
1/3–1/2 cup butter or
    margarine, melted

Grease a 9 x 13-inch pan. Sprinkle half of the cake mix evenly into bottom of pan. Spread pie filling evenly over cake mix. Cover with remaining cake mix. Drizzle butter over top. Bake for 47–52 minutes, or until light golden brown.

Sparkling Raspberry Cobbler

Makes 15–18 servings

Preheat oven to 350 degrees.

1 (21-ounce) can
    raspberry pie filling
1 yellow or white
    cake mix
1 (12-ounce) can lemon-
    lime soft drink

Pour pie filling into the bottom of a lightly greased 9 x 13-inch pan. Sprinkle the cake mix over top. Pour soft drink evenly over pie filling and cake mix. Bake for 47–52 minutes, or until light golden brown.

NOTE: Other berry pie fillings may be used.

Cherry-Pineapple Cobbler

Makes 15–18 servings

Preheat oven to 350 degrees.

1 yellow cake mix
1 (20-ounce) can
    crushed pineapple,
    with juice
1 (21-ounce) can
    cherry pie filling
1/4–1/2 cup butter or
    margarine, thinly
    sliced

Grease a 9 x 13-inch pan. Sprinkle half of the cake mix evenly into bottom of pan. Arrange pineapple over cake mix. Spread the pie filling over pineapple. Cover with remaining cake mix. Put butter slices over top. Bake for 48–53 minutes, or until light golden brown.

Chocolate Cherry Cobbler

Makes 15–18 servings

Preheat oven to 350 degrees.

1 chocolate cake mix
1 (20-ounce) can
    crushed pineapple,
    with juice
1 (21-ounce) can
    cherry pie filling
3/4 cup chopped pecans
1/2 cup butter or
    margarine, melted

Grease a 9 x 13-inch pan. Sprinkle half of the cake mix evenly into bottom of pan. Arrange the pineapple over cake mix. Spread pie filling over pineapple. Cover with the remaining cake mix and then sprinkle with the pecans. Drizzle the butter over top. Bake for 45–50 minutes, or until done.

Pumpkin Crunch

Makes 15–18 servings

Preheat oven to 350 degrees.

4 eggs, slightly beaten
1 cup sugar
2 teaspoons pumpkin
   pie spice
1 (12-ounce) can
   evaporated milk
1 teaspoon salt
1 (15-ounce) can
   pumpkin
1 box yellow or spice
   cake mix
1/2 cup butter or
   margarine, melted
1 cup chopped pecans
   or almonds
1 (8-ounce) container
   whipped topping

In a bowl, mix together the eggs, sugar, pumpkin pie spice, evaporated milk, salt, and pumpkin. Pour into a lightly greased 9 x 13-inch pan. Sprinkle cake mix evenly over pumpkin mixture. Drizzle the butter over the cake mix. Sprinkle nuts evenly over top. Bake for 50 minutes; let cool for 1 hour and then chill for at least 2 hours. Serve individual pieces with a dollop of whipped topping. Store in refrigerator.

Lemon Raspberry Trifle

Makes **15–18** *servings*

1 white or lemon
   cake mix
1 (14-ounce) can sweet-
   ened condensed milk
1 (6-ounce) container
   lemon yogurt
1/3 cup lemon juice
1½ teaspoons grated
   lemon peel
2 cups whipped topping
2 cups raspberries

Prepare and bake cake according to package directions in a
9 x 13-inch pan; let cool.

In a bowl, mix together the condensed milk, yogurt, lemon juice,
and lemon peel. Gently fold in the
whipped topping.

Crumble half of the cake into the
bottom of a trifle bowl. Spread half
of the yogurt mixture over cake.
Repeat layers. Garnish with the
raspberries. Refrigerate until ready
to serve.

NOTE: Try replacing the raspberries
with blueberries or strawberries.

Cherry Cheesecake Trifle

Makes 15–18 *servings*

1 white cake mix
1 (8-ounce) package
   cream cheese,
   softened
1 cup sour cream
½ cup milk
1 small box instant
   vanilla or cheesecake
   pudding
1 (8-ounce) container
   whipped topping
2 (21-ounce) cans
   cherry pie filling*

Prepare and bake cake according to package directions in a 9 x 13-inch pan; let cool.

In a bowl, mix together the cream cheese, sour cream, milk, and pudding mix until smooth and thick. Gently fold in the whipped topping.

Crumble half of the cake into the bottom of a trifle bowl. Spread half of the cream cheese mixture over cake. Spread 1 can of pie filling over cream cheese layer. Repeat layers. Refrigerate until ready to serve.

*Any flavor pie filling can be used in this recipe.

Double Berry Trifle

Makes 15–18 *servings*

1 white cake mix
2 small boxes instant
    vanilla or cheesecake
    pudding
4 cups milk
1 (21-ounce) can
    blueberry pie filling
1 (21-ounce) can
    cherry or raspberry
    pie filling
1 (12-ounce) container
    whipped topping
1/2 cup chopped nuts

Prepare and bake cake accord
ing to package directions in a
9 x 13-inch pan; let cool.

In a bowl, whisk together the
pudding mix and milk for 2 minutes. Chill at least 5 minutes to
set. Crumble half of cooled cake
into the bottom of a trifle bowl.
Spread half of pudding over cake.
Repeat layers. Spread blueberry
pie filling over pudding, followed
by the cherry or raspberry pie filling. Spread whipped topping over
top and then sprinkle with the nuts.
Refrigerate until ready to serve.

Cherry Crumb Cake

Makes 15–18 servings

1 yellow cake mix
2 small boxes instant
    vanilla pudding
4 cups milk
1 (20-ounce) can
    crushed pineapple,
    drained
1 (21-ounce) can
    cherry pie filling
1 (12-ounce) container
    whipped topping
1/2 cup chopped nuts

Prepare and bake cake according to package directions in a greased 9 x 13-inch pan; let cool.

In a bowl, whisk together the pudding mix and milk for 2 minutes. Chill at least 5 minutes to set. Crumble half of cooled cake into the bottom of a trifle bowl. Pour half of the pudding over top. Repeat layers. Spread the pineapple over top, followed by the pie filling. Spread whipped topping over pie filling. Sprinkle nuts over top. Refrigerate until ready to serve.

Butterfinger Crumb Cake

1 chocolate cake mix
2 small boxes instant
   vanilla pudding
4 cups milk
2 large Butterfinger
   candy bars, chopped
1 (12-ounce) container
   whipped topping

Prepare and bake cake according to package directions in a greased 9 x 13-inch pan; let cool.

In a bowl, whisk together the pudding mix and milk for 2 minutes. Chill at least 5 minutes to set. Pour half of the pudding into the bottom of a large glass bowl. Crumble half of cooled cake over top and gently press into pudding. Sprinkle one-third of the Butterfinger crumbs over the cake. Repeat layers. Spread whipped topping over top. Sprinkle remaining Butterfinger crumbs over whipped topping. Refrigerate until ready to serve.

Chocolate Lovers Crumb Cake

Makes 15–18 servings

1 chocolate cake mix
¾ cup semisweet
   chocolate chips
1 small box instant
   chocolate pudding
2 cups milk
1 cup hot fudge or
   caramel ice cream
   topping, divided
1 (12-ounce) container
   whipped topping,
   thawed
½ cup chopped nuts

Prepare cake mix according to package directions. Stir in the chocolate chips. Bake in a greased 9 x 13-inch pan; let cool.

In a bowl, whisk together the pudding mix and milk for 2 minutes. Chill at least 5 minutes to set. Pour pudding into the bottom of a large glass bowl. Crumble half of cooled cake over top and gently press into pudding. Drizzle ¾ cup hot fudge over the crumbs. Cover with remaining cake crumbs and then gently pat down. Spread whipped topping over top and refrigerate until ready to serve. Just before serving, drizzle with remaining hot fudge and sprinkle with chopped nuts.

Cheesecakes & Dessert Pizzas

Easy Cheesecake

1 yellow cake mix
2 (8-ounce) packages
    cream cheese,
    softened
½ cup sugar
1½ teaspoons vanilla,
    divided
2 eggs
¼ cup sour cream
2 squares unsweetened
    chocolate
3 tablespoons butter or
    margarine
2 tablespoons boiling
    water
1 cup powdered sugar

Preheat oven to 350 degrees.

Grease the bottom of a 9-inch springform pan; set aside. Prepare cake mix according to package directions. Pour half of the batter evenly into the greased pan. Bake for 20 minutes. Discard the extra batter or make a cake in a small round pan for snacking.

In a bowl, use an electric mixer to beat together the cream cheese, sugar, and ¾ teaspoon vanilla until smooth. Add the eggs one at a time, mixing at low speed after each addition just until blended. Stir in the sour cream. Pour mixture over cake.

Bake for 35 minutes, or until center is almost set. Run a knife around rim of pan to separate cake from side of pan.

Melt the chocolate and butter over low heat, stirring until smooth. Remove from heat. Add water, sugar, and vanilla; mix well. Spread over cooled cheesecake. Refrigerate at least 4 hours or overnight.

Pumpkin Cheesecake

Makes **16** *servings*

1 spice cake mix
1/2 cup butter or
 margarine, melted
4 eggs, divided
3 (8-ounce) packages
 cream cheese,
 softened
1 cup sugar
1 teaspoon vanilla
1 (15-ounce) can
 pumpkin
1 teaspoon cinnamon
1/2 teaspoon nutmeg
1/2 teaspoon allspice

Preheat oven to 325 degrees.

In a bowl, use a spoon to mix together the cake mix, butter, and 1 egg. Divide dough in half and then press into the bottom of two lightly greased pie pans.

In a separate bowl, mix together the cream cheese, sugar, vanilla, pumpkin, and spices. Mix in remaining eggs, one at a time. Pour half of filling over each crust. Bake together both cheesecakes for 50–55 minutes, or until the center is firm. Store in refrigerator.

Easy Cheesecake Bars

Makes 15–18 *servings*

Preheat oven to 350 degrees.

1 yellow cake mix
¹/₂ cup butter or
   margarine, melted
   and cooled
1 egg, beaten
1 pound powdered sugar
2 eggs, beaten
1 (8-ounce) package
   cream cheese,
   softened
1 teaspoon vanilla

In a bowl, mix together the cake mix, butter, and egg. Spread mixture into the bottom of a greased 9 x 13-inch pan.

In a separate bowl, mix together the powdered sugar, eggs, cream cheese, and vanilla until smooth. Spread mixture over bottom layer. Bake for 30–35 minutes.

Raspberry Cheesecake Bars

Makes 15–18 *servings*

1 white or yellow
   cake mix
1/2 cup butter or
   margarine, melted
4 eggs, divided
1 (12-ounce) jar
   seedless raspberry
   jam, divided
2 (8-ounce) packages
   cream cheese,
   softened
3/4 cup sugar
1/2 teaspoon vanilla
1/2 teaspoon grated
   lemon peel

Preheat oven to 350 degrees.

In a bowl, use a spoon to mix together the cake mix, butter, and 1 egg. Press dough into the bottom of a greased 9 x 13-inch pan. Stir jam until smooth. Spread half of the jam evenly over crust layer.

In a separate bowl, mix together the cream cheese, sugar, vanilla, and lemon peel. Beat in the remaining eggs one at a time. Pour mixture over jam layer. Bake for 25–35 minutes, or until golden brown and center is firm; let cool.

In a saucepan, heat remaining jam. Drizzle over cooled cheesecake. Chill for at least 3 hours or overnight. Store in refrigerator. Cut into bars before serving.

Blackberry Cheesecake Pudding Bars

Makes 15–18 servings

1 white cake mix
1/2 cup butter or
    margarine, melted
1 egg
1 (8-ounce) package
    cream cheese,
    softened
1 cup powdered sugar
1½ cups milk
1 small box instant
    cheesecake pudding
1 (8-ounce) container
    whipped topping
1 (21-ounce) can
    blackberry pie filling

Preheat oven to 350 degrees.

In a bowl, use a spoon to mix together the cake mix, butter, and egg. Press dough into a lightly greased 9 x 13-inch pan. Bake for 14–18 minutes, or until light golden brown around edges. Using a spoon, remove air pockets by pushing down evenly over entire hot crust; cool completely.

In a separate bowl, use an electric mixer to beat together the cream cheese and powdered sugar. Gradually beat in milk and pudding mix until smooth. Allow mixture to thicken in refrigerator for 5 minutes. Gently fold whipped topping into mixture with a spatula and then spread over the cooled crust. Spoon the pie filling evenly over top. Chill at least 2 hours before serving and then cut into bars. Store in refrigerator.

NOTE: You can also try using raspberry, blueberry, or cherry pie filling in place of the blackberry.

Chocolate Chip Cheesecake Bars

Makes **10–12** *servings*

1 white cake mix
½ cup flour
3 eggs, divided
⅓ cup vegetable oil
¾ cup chocolate chips
4 ounces cream cheese,
softened
½ cup sugar

Preheat oven to 350 degrees.

In a bowl, use a spoon to mix together the cake mix, flour, 2 eggs, and oil. Stir in the chocolate chips. Press half of the dough into a greased 8 x 8-inch pan.

In a separate bowl, use an electric mixer to beat together the cream cheese, sugar, and remaining egg until smooth. Spread mixture over bottom dough layer. Crumble remaining dough evenly over top. Bake for 24–28 minutes, or until light golden brown; cool completely and then cut into bars. Store in refrigerator.

Fruit Pizza

Makes **20** *servings*

1 white cake mix
1 egg
½ cup butter or
    margarine, melted
½ cup flour
¼ cup powdered sugar
1 (8-ounce) package
    cream cheese,
    softened
1 (8-ounce) container
    whipped topping
Sliced strawberries,
    bananas, kiwi, pine-
    apple, or peaches
Blueberries, grapes,
    raspberries,
    mandarin oranges,
    or grapes
Coconut (optional)

Preheat oven to 350 degrees.

In a bowl, use a spoon to mix together the cake mix, egg, and butter. Stir in the flour. Press dough in a thin layer to cover a lightly greased jelly roll pan or cookie sheet. Bake for 10–14 minutes, or until light golden brown around edges; cool completely.

In a separate bowl, mix together the powdered sugar, cream cheese, and whipped topping. Spread over cooled crust. Top with fruits of choice and sprinkle coconut over top, if desired. Store in refrigerator.

Chocolate
Peanut Butter Pizza

Makes **20** *servings*

1 chocolate cake mix
1 egg
½ cup butter or
    margarine, melted
½ cup flour
1 small box instant
    chocolate pudding
1½ cups milk
½ cup plain yogurt
⅓ cup peanut butter
3 Butterfinger bars,
    chopped (or Reese's
    Peanut Butter Cups)

Preheat oven to 350 degrees.

In a bowl, use a spoon to mix together the cake mix, egg, and butter. Stir in the flour. Press dough in a thin layer to cover a lightly greased jelly roll pan or cookie sheet. Bake for 10–14 minutes, or until light golden brown around edges; cool completely.

In a separate bowl, beat together the pudding mix, milk, yogurt, and peanut butter. Refrigerate for at least 5–10 minutes. Spread mixture over cooled cookie layer and then sprinkle the candy over top. Chill until ready to serve.

Peanut Butter–Caramel Apple Pizza

Makes 20 servings

1 white cake mix
1 egg
1/2 cup butter or
   margarine, melted
1/2 cup flour
1 (8-ounce) package
   cream cheese,
   softened
1/2 cup firmly packed
   brown sugar
1/4 cup creamy peanut
   butter
1/2 teaspoon vanilla
1 1/2 cups chopped
   apples*
1/3 cup caramel ice
   cream topping
3/4 cup chopped peanuts,
   unsalted

Preheat oven to 350 degrees.

In a bowl, use a spoon to mix together the cake mix, egg, and butter. Stir in the flour. Press dough in a thin layer to cover a lightly greased jelly roll pan or cookie sheet. Bake for 10–14 minutes, or until light golden brown around edges; cool completely.

In a separate bowl, use an electric mixer to beat together the cream cheese, brown sugar, peanut butter, and vanilla until smooth. Spread mixture over top of cooled crust. Sprinkle apple pieces over top.

Warm the caramel topping in the microwave for 30–45 seconds. Drizzle over apples. Sprinkle nuts over top. Store in refrigerator.

*Dip apple pieces in lemon juice to prevent them from browning.

Banana Split Pizza

Makes 20 *servings*

1 white or yellow
    cake mix
1 egg
$1/2$ cup butter or
    margarine, melted
$1/2$ cup flour
$1/4$ cup powdered sugar
1 (8-ounce) package
    cream cheese,
    softened
1 (8-ounce) container
    whipped topping
1 (8-ounce) can
    pineapple chunks,
    drained
2 bananas, thinly sliced
$1 1/2$ cups sliced
    strawberries
$1/2$ cup chopped nuts
Hot fudge and caramel
    ice cream toppings
    (optional)

Preheat oven to 350 degrees.

In a bowl, use a spoon to mix together the cake mix, egg, and butter. Stir in the flour. Press dough in a thin layer to cover a lightly greased jelly roll pan or cookie sheet. Bake for 10–14 minutes, or until light golden brown around edges; cool completely.

In a separate bowl, mix together the powdered sugar, cream cheese, and whipped topping. Spread mixture over crust. Top evenly with fruit and nuts. Drizzle ice cream toppings over top, if desired. Store in refrigerator.

Rocky Road Pizza

Makes 20 *servings*

1 chocolate cake mix
1 egg
½ cup butter or
    margarine, melted
2 cups mini
    marshmallows
1½ cups milk chocolate
    chips
¾ cup chopped nuts
½ cup caramel ice
    cream topping

Preheat oven to 350 degrees.

In a bowl, use a spoon to mix together the cake mix, egg, and butter. Press dough into a thin layer to cover a lightly greased jelly roll pan or cookie sheet. Bake for 10 minutes. Top hot crust evenly with marshmallows, chocolate chips, and nuts. Drizzle caramel topping over pizza. Return to oven for 3–5 minutes more to puff marshmallows and slightly melt the chocolate. Cool 10 minutes before serving.

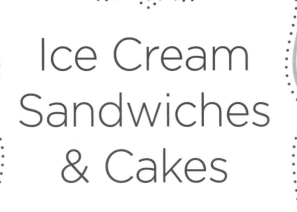

Ice Cream
Sandwiches
& Cakes

Easy Ice Cream Sandwiches

Makes 16–18
ice cream sandwiches

1 devil's food cake mix
½ cup oil
2 eggs
½ gallon vanilla ice cream, slightly softened

Preheat oven to 350 degrees.

In a bowl, use a spoon to mix together the cake mix, oil, and eggs. Drop 1-inch dough balls onto an ungreased cookie sheet. Bake for 8–10 minutes; cool on a wire rack. When cooled, place a scoop of ice cream between 2 cookies. Wrap tightly in plastic wrap and store in an airtight container in the freezer.

Strawberry Ice Cream Sandwiches

Makes 16–18
ice cream sandwiches

1 strawberry cake mix
⅓ cup oil
2 eggs
½ gallon strawberry, strawberry ripple, or vanilla ice cream

Preheat oven to 350 degrees.

In a bowl, use a spoon to mix together the cake mix, oil, and eggs. Drop 1-inch dough balls onto an ungreased cookie sheet. Bake for 8–12 minutes; cool on a wire rack. When cooled, place a scoop of ice cream between 2 cookies. Wrap tightly in plastic wrap and store in an airtight container in the freezer.

Tangy Ice Cream Sandwiches

Makes **16–18**
ice cream sandwiches

**1 lemon or orange
  cake mix**
1/3 cup vegetable oil
2 eggs
**1/2 gallon vanilla ice
  cream**

Preheat oven to 350 degrees.

In a bowl, use a spoon to mix together the cake mix, oil, and eggs. Drop 1-inch dough balls onto an ungreased cookie sheet. Bake for 8–12 minutes, or until light golden brown around edges. Leave cookies on pan for 2–3 minutes. Move to a wire rack to cool completely. When cooled, place a scoop of ice cream between 2 cookies. Wrap each sandwich tightly in plastic wrap and then store in an airtight container in the freezer.

Banana Split Ice Cream Cake

Makes **20** *servings*

1 yellow or white
    cake mix
1 egg
½ cup butter or
    margarine, melted
2 (½-gallon) boxes
    vanilla, chocolate,
    or strawberry ice
    cream, softened
1 (12-ounce) jar
    pineapple ice cream
    topping
1 (12-ounce) jar straw-
    berry or hot fudge
    ice cream topping
¾ cup chopped nuts
    (optional)
2 bananas, sliced

Preheat oven to 350 degrees.

In a bowl, use a spoon to mix together the cake mix, egg, and butter. Press dough into a lightly greased 9 x 13-inch pan. Bake for 7–10 minutes. Crust will not be cooked completely. Freeze for 1 hour.

Spread 1 box of ice cream evenly over the crust. Freeze for 1 hour. Spread pineapple topping over the ice cream. Spread second box of ice cream over the pineapple topping. Freeze 1–2 hours more. Spread the strawberry or hot fudge topping evenly over top, followed by the nuts, if desired. Cover and freeze at least 3 hours or overnight. Serve with freshly sliced bananas. Store in freezer.

NOTE: Two different flavors of ice cream can be used.

Butter Pecan Ice Cream Cake

Makes **20** servings

**1 yellow, white,
  or butter pecan
  cake mix**
1 egg
**1/2 cup butter or
  margarine, melted**
**2 (1/2-gallon) boxes
  butter pecan ice
  cream, softened**
**1 (12-ounce) jar
  butterscotch or
  caramel ice cream
  topping**
3/4 cup chopped pecans

Preheat oven to 350 degrees.

In a bowl, use a spoon to mix together the cake mix, egg, and butter. Press dough into a lightly greased 9 x 13-inch pan. Bake for 7–10 minutes. Crust will not be cooked completely; cool.

Spread both boxes of ice cream over the crust. Spread ice cream topping over top, followed by the pecans. Cover and freeze 4 hours or overnight. Store in freezer.

Peanut Butter Ice Cream Cake

Makes 20 servings

1 yellow or white
    cake mix
1 egg
½ cup butter or
    margarine, melted
2 (½-gallon) boxes
    vanilla or chocolate
    ice cream, softened
⅔ cup peanut butter
1 cup corn syrup
¾ cup chopped nuts

Preheat oven to 350 degrees.

In a bowl, use a spoon to mix together the cake mix, egg, and butter. Press dough into a lightly greased 9 x 13-inch pan. Bake for 7–10 minutes. Crust will not be cooked completely; cool.

Spread both boxes of ice cream over crust.

In a small microwave-safe bowl, soften the peanut butter in the microwave for 10–30 seconds on high. Stir in corn syrup. Spread mixture over the ice cream. Sprinkle the nuts over top. Cover and freeze at least 4 hours before serving. Store in freezer.

Strawberry Ice Cream Cake

Makes **20** *servings*

1 yellow, white, or
    strawberry cake mix
1 egg
1/2 cup butter or
    margarine, melted
2 (1/2-gallon) boxes
    strawberry,
    strawberry ripple,
    or strawberry
    cheesecake ice
    cream, softened
1 (12-ounce) jar
    strawberry ice
    cream topping
Strawberries, sliced
    (optional)

Preheat oven to 350 degrees.

In a bowl, use a spoon to mix together the cake mix, egg, and butter. Press dough into a lightly greased 9 x 13-inch pan. Bake for 7–10 minutes. Crust will not be cooked completely; cool.

Spread both boxes of ice cream over crust. Spread strawberry topping over top. Cover and freeze at least 4 hours before serving. Serve with freshly sliced strawberries, if desired. Store in freezer.

Family
Favorites &
Holiday Fun

Apple Spice Cupcakes

Makes 24 *cupcakes*

1 spice cake mix
3 eggs
1¼ cups water
⅓ cup applesauce
1 cup chopped apples
1 container vanilla
    or cream cheese
    frosting

Preheat oven to 350 degrees. Lightly grease cups of a muffin pan and set aside.

In a bowl, mix together the cake mix, eggs, water, and applesauce until smooth. Stir in the apples. Fill muffin cups about two-thirds full and bake for 18–23 minutes. Remove cupcakes from pan to cool completely. Top cupcakes with frosting.

Carrot Spice Cupcakes

Makes 24 *cupcakes*

1 spice cake mix
1¼ cups shredded
    carrot
½ teaspoon cinnamon
½ cup chopped or
    grated nuts
1 container white
    or cream cheese
    frosting

Preheat oven to 350 degrees. Lightly grease cups of a muffin pan and set aside.

Prepare cake according to package directions. Stir in the carrot, cinnamon, and nuts. Fill muffin cups about two-thirds full. Bake for 18–23 minutes. Remove from pan and to cool completely. Top cupcakes with frosting.

Boysenberry Delight Cupcakes

Makes **24** *cupcakes*

1 white cake mix
1 (6-ounce) container
 boysenberry yogurt

Frosting
1 (8-ounce) container
 whipped topping
1 (6-ounce) container
 boysenberry yogurt

Preheat oven to 350 degrees. Lightly grease cups of a muffin pan and set aside.

Prepare cake according to package directions. Fold in the yogurt. Fill muffin cups about two-thirds full and bake for 18–23 minutes. Chill cupcakes for at least 3 hours.

In a bowl, combine the whipped topping and yogurt. Top cupcakes with frosting just before serving.

Quick Pumpkin Cupcakes

Makes **24** *cupcakes*

1 spice cake mix
2 eggs
1 cup pumpkin
⅓ cup water
1 container cream
 cheese or vanilla
 frosting
Candy pumpkins
 (optional)

Preheat oven to 350 degrees. Lightly grease cups of a muffin pan and set aside.

In a bowl, mix together the cake mix, eggs, pumpkin, and water. Fill muffin cups two-thirds full. Bake for 15–20 minutes; let cool. Top cupcakes with frosting. If desired, place a candy pumpkin on top of frosted cupcake.

Caramel Surprise Cupcakes

Makes 24 cupcakes

1 yellow or white
    cake mix
1 cup butterscotch or
    chocolate chips
24 caramels,
    unwrapped*
1 container chocolate or
    white frosting

Preheat oven to 350 degrees. Lightly grease cups of a muffin pan and set aside.

Prepare cake according to package directions. Stir in butterscotch or chocolate chips. Fill muffin cups about one-third full and set unused batter aside. Bake for 5 minutes. Place a caramel in the center of each cupcake. Top with remaining cake batter to fill muffin cups about two-thirds full. Bake for 10–14 minutes more, or until done. Remove from pan and let cool completely. Top cupcakes with frosting.

*Miniature chocolate peanut butter cups or individual Rolos can be substituted.

Cream-Filled Cupcakes

Makes 24 cupcakes

1 strawberry or
   lemon cake mix*
1 (8-ounce) package
   cream cheese,
   softened
1 egg
2 cups powdered sugar
1 container vanilla
   or cream cheese
   frosting

Preheat oven to 350 degrees. Line cups of a muffin pan with cupcake liners and set aside.

Prepare cake according to package directions. Fill liners about half full.

In a bowl, use an electric mixer to beat together the cream cheese, egg, and powdered sugar. Place a tablespoon of cream cheese filling in the center of each cupcake. Bake for 18–23 minutes. Remove cupcakes from pan and cool completely. Top cupcakes with frosting.

*Any flavor cake mix can be used for this recipe for endless possibilities.

Ice Cream Cone Cupcakes

Makes 30 cupcake cones

1 chocolate cake mix
1¼ cups water
¼ cup vegetable oil
¼ cup applesauce
2 large eggs
30 flat-bottom
    ice cream cones
1 container frosting,
    any flavor
Candy sprinkles
    (optional)

Preheat oven to 350 degrees.

In a bowl, mix together the cake mix, water, oil, applesauce, and eggs until smooth. Fill each cone with about 2½ tablespoons batter. Place upright cones about 3 inches apart on an ungreased baking sheet or in a muffin pan. Bake for 25–30 minutes; cool completely.

Soften the frosting in the microwave on high for 10 seconds. Stir and then spread evenly over cupcakes. Place candy sprinkles on top, if desired.

Delicious Dirt

Makes 15–18 *servings*

1 devil's food cake mix
1 (8-ounce) package
    cream cheese,
    softened
3½ cups milk
2 small boxes instant
    chocolate pudding
1 (8-ounce) container
    whipped topping
½ package Oreo
    cookies, crushed

Preheat oven to 350 degrees.

Prepare and bake cake according to package directions; let cool. Crumble cake into a large bowl.

In a separate bowl, use an electric mixer to beat the cream cheese until smooth. Add the milk and pudding mix, blending until thickened. Gently fold the whipped topping into the pudding mixture. Spoon the mixture over the cake crumbs in the bowl. Sprinkle cookies over top. Store in the refrigerator.

NOTE: Sprinkle some gummy worms over the top for an extra fun addition. This recipe can also be prepared in individual cups.

Strawberry Parfaits

Makes 12 large parfaits

1 strawberry cake mix
2 eggs
1/2 cup butter or
    margarine, softened
1 cup white chocolate
    chips
2 small boxes instant
    vanilla pudding
4 cups milk
1 (12–16-ounce)
    container whipped
    topping
Strawberries, sliced
    (optional)

Preheat oven to 350 degrees.

In a bowl, use a spoon to mix together the cake mix, eggs, and butter. Stir in the white chocolate chips. Press dough into a greased 9 x 13-inch pan. Bake for 14–18 minutes, or until light golden brown around edges; let cool uncovered for 1–2 hours and then crumble.

In a separate bowl, whisk together the pudding mix and milk for 2 minutes. Chill 5 minutes to set.

In parfait glasses, layer cake crumbs, pudding, whipped topping, and strawberries. Repeat for three layers.

Strawberry Sweetheart Cake

Makes 15–18 servings

1 French vanilla
   cake mix
1 large carton frozen
   sweetened sliced
   strawberries, thawed
1 small box instant
   French vanilla or
   cheesecake pudding
2 cups milk
1 (8-ounce) container
   whipped topping
Fresh strawberries

Preheat oven to 350 degrees.

Prepare and bake cake in a 9 x 13-inch pan according to package directions; let cool and then refrigerate for several hours. Just before serving, poke holes at 1-inch intervals over top of cake using a wooden spoon handle. Spoon strawberries and juice evenly over top of cake, allowing mixture to soak into holes.

In a bowl, mix together the pudding mix and milk. Spread over the strawberries. Spread whipped topping over the pudding. Slice fresh strawberries and arrange on top of cake in the shape of a heart.

Valentine Heart Cookies

Makes 30 *cookies*

1 cherry chip cake mix
2 eggs
$\frac{1}{3}$ cup vegetable oil
1 container white
    frosting
Red food coloring and
    sprinkles (optional)

Preheat oven to 350 degrees.

In a bowl, use a spoon to mix together the cake mix, eggs, and oil. Scoop 1-inch balls of dough onto a greased cookie sheet and then form each ball into the shape of a heart. Bake for 8–12 minutes, or until light golden brown. Top with frosting that has been mixed with a little red food coloring, if desired, and sprinkles.

American Flag Cake

Makes 15–18 *servings*

1 white cake mix
1 small box strawberry
    gelatin
1 cup boiling water
$\frac{1}{2}$ cup cold water
2 cups whipped topping
1$\frac{1}{2}$ cups sliced
    strawberries
2 bananas, sliced
$\frac{1}{2}$ cup blueberries

Preheat oven to 350 degrees.

Prepare cake and bake in a 9 x 13-inch pan according to package directions. Poke hot cake at 1-inch intervals with a fork. Dissolve gelatin in the boiling water and then stir in the cold water. Slowly drizzle gelatin over cake to let it soak in. Chill for 3 hours. Spread with whipped topping. Arrange the strawberries and bananas into stripes and the blueberries in one corner as the stars.

Red, White, and Blue Poke Cake

Makes 15–18 *servings*

1 white cake mix
2 cups milk
1 small box instant
  cheesecake or vanilla
  pudding
1 (21-ounce) can
  cherry pie filling
1 (21-ounce) can
  blueberry pie filling
1 (12-ounce) container
  whipped topping

Prepare cake and bake in a 9 x 13-inch pan according to package directions; let cool. With the handle of a wooden spoon, poke holes at 1-inch intervals clear through the cake.

In a bowl, use a wire whisk to beat together the pudding mix and milk for 2 minutes. Chill for at least 5 minutes to set. Pour pudding over cake. Spread cherry pie filling over pudding. Spread blueberry pie filling over top. Cover with the whipped topping. Refrigerate at least 2 hours before serving. Store in refrigerator.

Jack-o-Lantern Cake

Makes 25 *servings*

2 cake mixes, any flavor
2 (16-ounce) containers
    white frosting
Orange, green, and
    black food coloring
1 Hostess Ho-Ho (or
    similar cake-roll
    snack item)

Prepare and bake each cake in greased Bundt cake pans according to package directions; remove from pans and cool completely.

Color most of the frosting a deep orange, reserving about ½ cup. Color half of the reserved frosting green and the other half black, or use dark chocolate fudge frosting instead. Place 1 cake upside down (rounded side on the bottom) on a platter; frost only the flat top. Place remaining cake flat-side down on top of first cake. Frost entire cake with the orange frosting, spreading it in up and down motions with a spatula to create the pumpkin's curves. Insert the Ho-Ho in the middle of the top cake and frost green to make the stem. Use the black frosting to make the eyes, nose, and mouth.

NOTE: Black rope licorice may also be used to make a face!

Black Cat Cookies

Makes 30 *cookies*

³/₄ **cup chunky peanut butter**
2 eggs
¹/₃ **cup water**
1 chocolate cake mix
Sugar
Plain M&Ms
Red Hots

Preheat oven to 350 degrees.

In a bowl, beat together the peanut butter, eggs, and water. Gradually add the cake mix and blend well. Form dough into 1-inch balls. Place on a lightly greased cookie sheet and flatten balls with bottom of a glass dipped in some sugar. Pinch out two ears at top of each cookie. Add M&Ms as eyes and a Red Hot for the nose. Press fork into the sides of the cat face to form some whiskers. Bake for 8–10 minutes; let cool.

Halloween Candy Cake

Makes 15–18 servings

1 yellow cake mix
¾ cup chopped unsalted
    roasted peanuts
1 cup water
⅓ cup oil
2 eggs

Topping
1 container vanilla
    frosting
⅓ cup peanut butter
½ cup unsalted roasted
    peanuts, chopped
1 Butterfinger bar,
    chopped
16 candy pumpkins

Preheat oven to 350 degrees. Grease a 9 x 13-inch pan; set aside.

In a bowl, combine all cake ingredients using an electric mixer on slow speed. Pour into the prepared pan. Bake for 30–40 minutes, or until a toothpick inserted into the center comes out clean; let cool completely.

In a separate bowl, mix together the frosting and peanut butter until smooth. Spread evenly over cake. Sprinkle with peanuts and Butterfinger pieces. Arrange the candy pumpkins on top.

Halloween Spider Cake

Makes 12–15 *servings*

1 small box lime gelatin
1 white cake mix
Blue food coloring
Chocolate frosting
8 pieces black licorice
2 large green gumballs

Prepare lime gelatin as directed on the box; refrigerate until set. Chop gelatin into small pieces and chill until ready to use.

Prepare cake according to package directions. Bake in two greased 9-inch round cake pans.

Cut a circle out of the center of 1 layer of cake; set aside for the head. Fill the hole with the gelatin pieces. Lay the other cake on top. Place the small cake circle vertically against the round body of spider. Add blue food coloring to chocolate frosting until black in color; cover entire cake with the frosting. Use black licorice as legs on each side of the spider's body and use the gumballs for the eyes.

Thanksgiving Pumpkin Bars

Makes **15–18** *servings*

1 yellow cake mix, 1 cup
   reserved for topping
1/2 cup butter or
   margarine, melted
3 eggs, divided
1 (29-ounce) can
   pumpkin
2/3 cup milk
1 cup sugar
1 teaspoon cinnamon
1/2 teaspoon nutmeg
1/2 teaspoon ginger
1/2 teaspoon salt

Topping
1 cup reserved cake mix
2 tablespoons sugar
1/4 cup butter or
   margarine

Preheat oven to 350 degrees.

In a bowl, combine the cake mix, butter, and 1 egg. Press dough into a greased 9 x 13-inch pan; set aside.

In a separate bowl, mix together the remaining eggs, pumpkin, milk, sugar, spices, and salt until smooth. Pour over crust.

In another bowl, mix together the reserved cake mix and sugar; cut in margarine until crumbly. Sprinkle over filling. Bake for 50 minutes, or until a knife inserted into the center comes out clean.

Christmas Rainbow Poke Cake

Makes 15–18 *servings*

1 white cake mix
1 small box strawberry
   gelatin
2 cups boiling water,
   divided
½ cup cold water,
   divided
1 small box lime gelatin
1 (12-ounce) container
   whipped topping

Preheat oven to 350 degrees.

Prepare cake mix according to package directions. Pour batter into two 8- or 9-inch round pans and bake as directed; cool 10 minutes. Remove from pans and cool completely. Place cake layers, top sides up, back in the two clean pans. With a fork, poke holes at 1-inch intervals through both cakes. Dissolve strawberry gelatin into 1 cup boiling water. Mix ¼ cup cold water into gelatin mixture. Spoon over 1 layer of cake. Repeat with lime gelatin and spoon over opposite layer. Refrigerate 3–4 hours or overnight. Dip one pan into warm water for 10 seconds; invert onto a platter. Spread some of the whipped topping over top. Invert the second layer onto the first layer. Frost with remaining whipped topping. Refrigerate until ready to serve.

Index

Metric Conversion Chart					
Volume Measurements		Weight Measurements		Temperature Conversion	
U.S.	Metric	U.S.	Metric	Fahrenheit	Celsius
1 teaspoon	5 ml	1/2 ounce	15 g	250	120
1 tablespoon	15 ml	1 ounce	30 g	300	150
1/4 cup	60 ml	3 ounces	90 g	325	160
1/3 cup	75 ml	4 ounces	115 g	350	180
1/2 cup	125 ml	8 ounces	225 g	375	190
2/3 cup	150 ml	12 ounces	350 g	400	200
3/4 cup	175 ml	1 pound	450 g	425	220
1 cup	250 ml	2 1/4 pounds	1 kg	450	230